Cambodia

Cambodia

BY WIL MARA

Enchantment of the World™
Second Series

CHILDREN'S PRESS®

An Imprint of Scholastic Inc.

Frontispiece: **National Museum, Phnom Penh**

Consultant: Jennifer Goodlander, PhD, Assistant Professor, Southeast Asian and ASEAN Studies, School of Global & International Studies, Indiana University Bloomington, Bloomington, Indiana
Please note: All statistics are as up-to-date as possible at the time of publication.

Book production by The Design Lab

Library of Congress Cataloging-in-Publication Data
Names: Mara, Wil, author.
Title: Cambodia / by Wil Mara.
Description: New York : Children's Press, an imprint of Scholastic Inc.,
   [2017] | Includes bibliographical references and index.
Identifiers: LCCN 2016054363 | ISBN 9780531235737 (library binding : alk.
   paper)
Subjects: LCSH: Cambodia—Juvenile literature.
Classification: LCC DS554.3 .M37 2017 | DDC 959.6—dc23
LC record available at https://lccn.loc.gov/2016054363

33614080406910

1 2 3 4 5 6 7 8 9 10 R 27 26 25 24 23 22 21 20 19 18

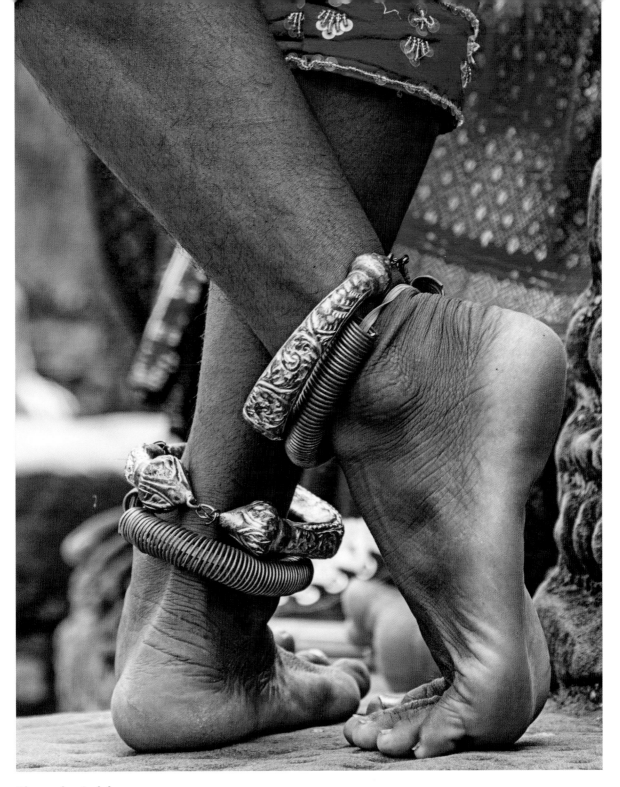

Khmer classical dancer

Contents

Left to right: **Tonle Sap Lake, waterfall, selling doughnuts, floating village, Buddhist monks**

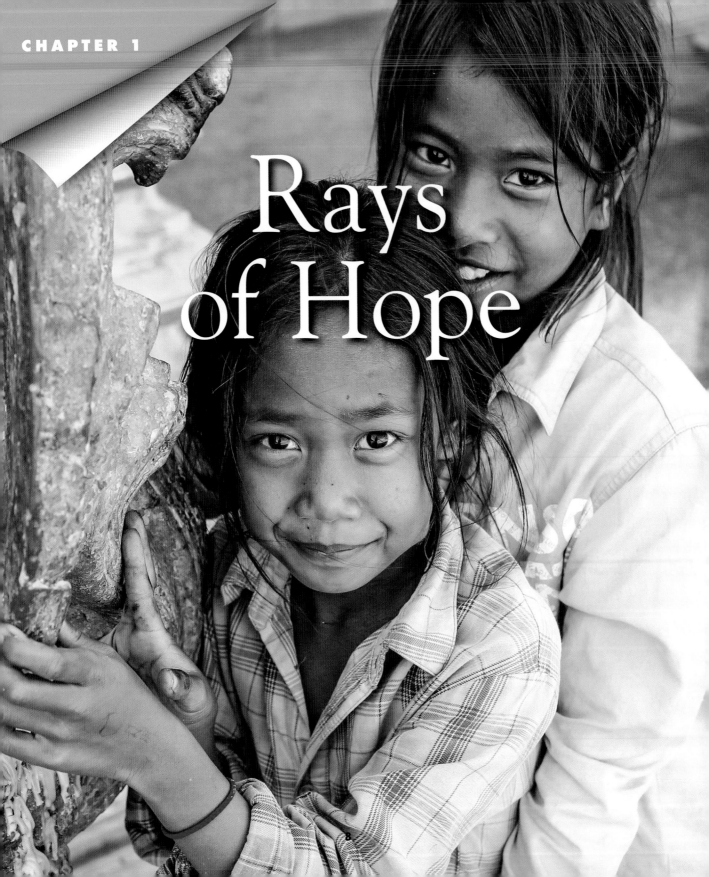

CHAPTER 1

Rays of Hope

TWELVE-YEAR-OLD NISAY AND HIS YOUNGER SISTER Kalliyann play along the river delta at the edge of their village. Their family has lived here for generations, as have many other families in the area. The people here are farmers and fishers, living simple lives and enjoying simple pleasures. They respect and rely upon each other. There is trust, safety, and happiness. But Nisay and Kalliyann are hoping for more.

They both go to school. It is not a large school—just one room in a hut about a mile away. And they have to walk there every day. It's not that the walk is so bad—the weather is always warm, and it's sunny except during the rainy season. Plus, they walk with their friends, which makes it a lot more fun. But their teacher doesn't always show up, which means

Opposite: **Girls in southern Cambodia. More than three out of every ten Cambodians are under age fifteen.**

Karaoke is extremely popular among young Cambodians.

they have to walk all the way back home again without having learned anything. They both like to learn; they believe knowledge gives them strength.

They have an uncle, Heng, and an aunt, Seyha, who live in Cambodia's capital city of Phnom Penh. Heng works as an IT tech, and Seyha is a restaurant manager. They both make good money; very good money compared to what people make in work found around the village. They own their own car and their own home. They go shopping on the weekends, and sometimes see a movie or go sing karaoke.

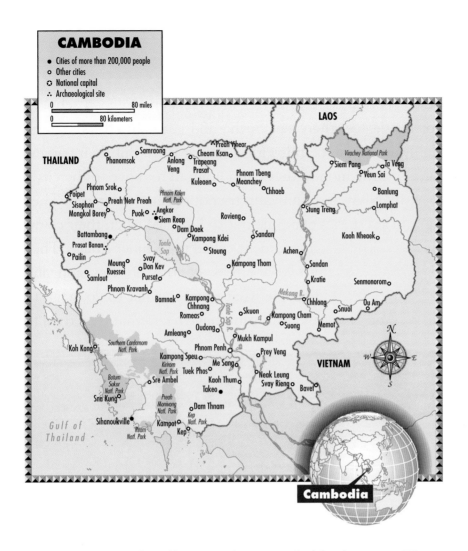

To Nisay and Kalliyann, this sounds like heaven. There have been times when they've had to stop going to school for a while in order to help out their family. They have both become good at farming and fishing, but they're not interested in doing either for the rest of their lives. Uncle Heng and Aunt Seyha tell them the only way they're going to get out of the village is through education. Uncle Heng tells the story of how his family took a big chance and moved to Phnom Penh when he was just a boy. His parents wanted to give him the best opportunity for a better life. He went to good schools, got his degree, then met Seyha and got married. Nisay and Kalliyann dream of following a similar path. But their parents have so little money, they cannot afford to move to the city.

Still, Nisay and Kalliyann try not to get discouraged. They have heard stories of a time not so long ago when their country was ruled by a government called the Khmer Rouge. They closed down many schools; took control of television and radio stations; told people what to wear, what to do, what to think. And Nisay and Kalliyann have heard that they tried to

A woman walks along train tracks in rural Cambodia. More than three-quarters of Cambodians live in rural areas.

get rid of all the people who wouldn't obey them. Some were forced out of the country. Others were killed. Their mother says she had an older brother, Makara, who was killed by the Khmer Rouge. She cries when she talks about him. Nisay and Kalliyann never knew him, but they still feel sad.

Their parents tell them that the government in charge of Cambodia today is a little better. Roads and bridges are being repaired, jobs are available, education is improving. They hope the situation in Cambodia will continue to get better so one day the country will be a place where everyone can have good jobs, nice homes, and happy futures.

Looking into the rippling waters of a river that has sustained their family for hundreds of years, Nisay and Kalliyann hope so, too.

Many Cambodians feel increasingly optimistic about their country's future. The poverty rate has fallen dramatically in recent years, with less than 20 percent of Cambodians now living in poverty.

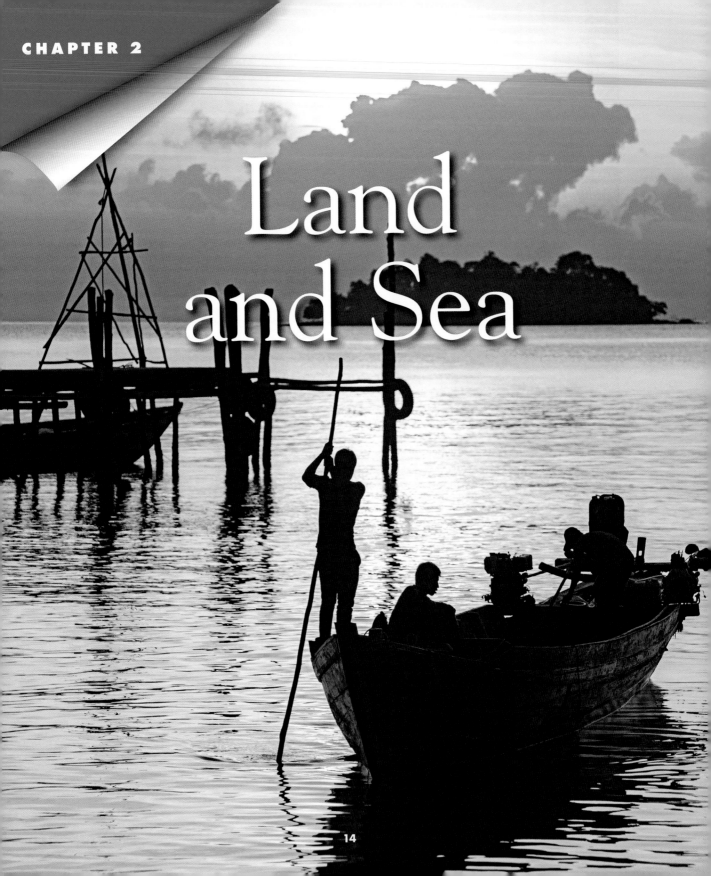

CHAPTER 2

Land and Sea

CAMBODIA IS LOCATED IN SOUTHEAST ASIA. IT falls entirely within a geographical band known as a tropical zone. The tropical zone is known for its heat and humidity, home to the steamiest places in the world.

Cambodia has three countries as neighbors—Thailand to the northwest, Laos to the northeast, and Vietnam to the east, southeast, and south. Most of Cambodia's southwestern border is shoreline, which meets with the Gulf of Thailand for about 275 miles (443 kilometers). Cambodia is a relatively small nation, with a total area of 69,898 square miles (181,035 sq km), roughly the same size as the U.S. state of Oklahoma.

Opposite: **A man guides a boat into the Gulf of Thailand, off Cambodia's southwestern coast.**

Bokor Mountain rises near the coast in southern Cambodia. Its higher elevation makes it a cooler retreat from the steamier lowlands.

Topography

The northeastern and southwestern parts of Cambodia are the areas with the highest elevation. The land gradually gets lower until it reaches the massive Tonle Sap Lake and its surrounding valley, which runs through the heart of the nation. Tonle Sap Lake is fed primarily by the Tonle Sap River. To the east is the Mekong River and its surrounding lowlands. The Mekong Delta extends south through Vietnam to the South China Sea. The Tonle Sap and Mekong lowland regions make up the largest part of the country. The land here is mostly flat plains.

The Tonle Sap Basin and the Mekong Delta are surrounded by mountain ranges—the Cardamom Mountains to the west, the Damrei Mountains to the southwest, and the Dangrek

Cambodia's Geographic Features

Area: 69,898 square miles (181,035 sq km)

Highest Elevation: Phnom Aural, at 5,948 feet (1,813 m)

Lowest Elevation: Sea level along the coast

Longest River: Mekong, 2,703 miles (4,350 km) long, 302 miles (486 km) of which is in Cambodia

Largest Lake: Tonle Sap Lake, 1,042 square miles (2,699 sq km)

Average Daily High Temperature: In Phnom Penh, 95.5°F (35°C) in April, 87°F (31°C) in December

Average Daily Low Temperature: In Phnom Penh, 78°F (25.5°C) in April, 71°F (22°C) in December

Highest Recorded Temperature: 108.7°F (42.6°C) at Preah Vihear, on April 15, 2016

Lowest Recorded Temperature: 46°F (8°C) in the Emerald Valley near Bokor on May 13, 1967

Rainiest Month: September in Phnom Penh, 13 inches (33 cm)

Driest Month: January in Phnom Penh, 0.55 inches (1.4 cm)

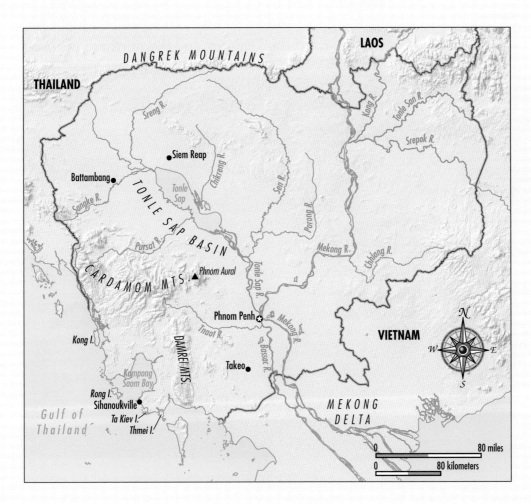

Mountains to the north. Elevated land areas to the east and northeast merge with the Central Highlands of Vietnam.

The Damrei and Cardamom ranges are bordered to the west by a coastal plain that includes Kampong Saom Bay, which faces the Gulf of Thailand. The Dangrek Mountains are located at the northern rim of the Tonle Sap Basin and possess particularly steep cliffs and ledges. This range faces southward and is part of the southern edge of Thailand's Khorat Plateau. A main road that runs through the Dangrek Mountains connects northwestern Cambodia with Thailand. Between the most westerly parts of the Dangrek and the northerly sections

Mist often hangs among the mountains in the Areng Valley in southwestern Cambodia.

of the Cardamom ranges lies an extension of the Tonle Sap Basin that merges into the lowlands in Thailand.

Many waterfalls form as streams tumble down Cambodia's mountains.

Islands

Cambodia includes about sixty islands off the southwestern coast in the Gulf of Thailand. Most of them are within easy reach of the shore. Many of these places look like the perfect island paradise. They feature sandy beaches, waving palm trees, lush plant life, and blue skies above bath-warm waters. These islands are remote and peaceful. Most are inhabited, although some are home to only a small number of people. Cambodia's largest island is Kong, which lies off the western coast. This hilly island is home to several small fishing villages.

Bright Lights, Big Cities

The largest city in Cambodia by population is the nation's capital, Phnom Penh, with about 1.5 million residents. Takeo is the second most populous city in Cambodia, with about 850,000 residents. It is the capital city of the Takeo Province, which is located along Cambodia's southern border. Takeo is known for its many ancient sites that were constructed around the sixth and seventh centuries. The word *city* is somewhat misleading regarding Takeo, since much of it is rural and remains undeveloped. Nevertheless, these rural areas are particularly beautiful. Takeo is in the heart of the region known as Water Chenla, where there are many lakes, rivers, and other waterways.

Sihanoukville (below) is Cambodia's third-largest city in terms of population, with just about 300,000 residents. Like Takeo, it is the key city within a province that bears the same name. It is located along the south-

western coast, and it has some of the most beautiful beaches in the nation. It is the largest seaside town in all of Cambodia, and a jumping off point for visiting Cambodia's many islands. Sihanoukville has a strong economy, with many tourist jobs, a broad factory base, and a thriving agricultural community. It is also a center for education: About one in four residents is a student.

Battambang is the nation's fourth-largest city, home to about 250,000 residents. The city is renowned for its beautifully preserved architecture from the French-colonial era (above). During that time, the nation was an economic hub, and the French made a point of improving the city. Today, Battambang is hugely popular with tourists. It offers a little of everything—bustling city life, family fun, and the beauty of rural areas that are nearby.

Tourists have flocked to islands such as Rong, Thmei, and Ta Kiev in recent times. The islands offer a little of everything. Some are modern, with restaurants, boating opportunities, Internet service, and private bungalows. Others are simpler, with huts standing right by the shore and a hammock strung between two trees.

Waterways

The main waterway in Cambodia is Tonle Sap Lake, which is fed into by the Tonle Sap River. The Tonle Sap, along with

Restaurants and shops line a beach on Rong, Cambodia's second-largest island.

Fishing boats on the Mekong River in Phnom Penh. The Mekong is the longest river in Southeast Asia.

numerous other waterways, is part of the Mekong River system. The Mekong is one of the most important waterways in all of southeastern Asia. It is the twelfth-longest river in the world, flowing 2,703 miles (4,350 km), about the distance from New York to Los Angeles, California. It begins high in the mountains of China and flows south through Myanmar (also known as Burma), Laos, Thailand, Cambodia, and Vietnam, all the way to the South China Sea. Although parts of the Mekong are difficult to navigate, it acts as one of the main trade routes between these nations.

There is significant variation in how much water flows in the Mekong, depending on the season. These variations affect the Tonle Sap and its tributaries as well. In the spring months, during the rainy season, river and streambeds will be inundated with more water than they can handle. Flooding is common, rendering much of the surrounding land unsuitable for agriculture. But this increase in water volume also has its value, as the Tonle Sap provides Cambodia with about two-thirds of its water supply.

Most other major waterways in Cambodia connect with the Tonle Sap system, particularly those that flow down from the east. Some rivers in the southwest empty directly into the Gulf of Thailand.

The size of Tonle Sap Lake changes dramatically depending on the season. The lake is about 22 miles (35 km) wide in the dry season. It grows to about 65 miles (105 km) wide in the rainy season, flooding nearby forests and fields.

Climate

In Cambodia, it is warm all year long. Cambodia's weather is greatly affected by seasonal winds, called monsoons. During the spring and summer months, these winds blow northwest from the Indian Ocean, carrying with them moisture that produces heavy rainfall and high humidity. Then, from mid-autumn to late winter, the winds change direction and roll down from the northeastern areas. This shift brings drier conditions and cooler temperatures. The basin area around Tonle Sap Lake is not as affected by these seasonal changes as other parts of the country.

Cows and people share a beach on a sunny day in Sihanoukville.

The hottest period in Cambodia is usually March through May. At this time, the monsoon winds from the southeast are reaching their peak, and the land is hammered with rain and increased humidity. Daily temperatures during this time can reach as high as 100 degrees Fahrenheit (38 degrees Celsius). In December and January, the dry air dispels much of the humidity and daytime temperatures are less likely to reach 90°F (32°C).

Rainfall also varies by geographic location and elevation. The nation as a whole receives around 40 to 60 inches (100 to 150 centimeters), with the region closest to the Gulf of Thailand getting the greatest amounts. The higher elevations get the most rain, some enduring as much as 150 inches (380 cm) or more in a single year.

The streets in Phnom Penh frequently flood after heavy rains.

CHAPTER 3

All Things Wild and Free

CAMBODIA IS HOME TO A GREAT VARIETY OF PLANTS and animals. The climate and environment is ideal for thousands of species, some of which are found nowhere else in the world. Interference from humankind has done damage over the years, but there are currently more efforts to right those wrongs than ever before.

Mammals

More than two hundred species of mammals live in Cambodia, from the tiny mouse deer to the fearsome tiger. The country is also home to giant creatures such as the Asian elephant, apes called gibbons that usually get around by swinging through the trees, and charming Irrawaddy dolphins, which live in the Mekong. Mammals can be found in every ecological niche, from highlands to lowlands and everywhere in between. Some species live only in one place, like the Tonle Sap Lake area, while others are widespread throughout Asia.

Opposite: **A misty bamboo forest in southern Cambodia. Bamboo grows throughout the country.**

In parts of Cambodia, furry mammals fill the air at night. Cambodia is home to more than two dozen different bat species. These include the lesser false vampire bat. It has a

Two flying foxes roost on a tree during the daytime.

Mini Mammal

The mouse deer is the smallest known mammal in the world that has hooves. When you think of a hoofed mammal, images of deer, antelope, horses, and perhaps even giraffes may come to mind—all creatures of fairly large sizes. Not the mouse deer, however. Adults average no more than around 20 inches (51 cm) long and weigh about 5 pounds (2 kilograms). That's about the size of a house cat. The mouse deer is a delicate-looking animal, with large round eyes, dark brown fur, and spindly legs. The mouse deer is clever and has learned to avoid being eaten by wild cats and other creatures. Its range extends well beyond Cambodia into many of its neighboring countries.

A Creature Most Rare

Cambodia's national animal is the kouprey, an oxlike mammal found in the wooded areas of northern Cambodia, as well as parts of adjacent Thailand, Vietnam, and Laos. It has a heavy body that is in startling contrast to its fairly narrow legs, humped back, and horns. Both males and females have horns. The male's horns point forward and upward, while the female's are spiral. Koupreys are herbivores, preferring to feed on grasses.

As the forests and grasslands where koupreys live have been destroyed, their numbers have dwindled. Today, experts estimate that there are probably no more than fifty mature koupreys in the world, and they may already be extinct. Koupreys are shy and secretive, and the last time one was actually seen in the wild was in 1988.

wingspan of about 12 inches (30 cm). Thousands of them live together in caves, abandoned buildings, and trees. They feed during the night on whatever insects they can catch. Despite its name, it does not attack humans and suck their blood. Cambodia is also known for its flying foxes. These reddish, woolly creatures are among the world's largest bats, with wings often 4 feet (1.2 meters) across. They eat flowers, nectar, and fruit, feeding on figs, mangoes, bananas, and more.

Birds

Cambodia is home to more than 550 bird species. Many are waterbirds, such as herons, pelicans, ducks, and cormorants. Grouse and pheasants live in the grasslands. The spectacular

The green peafowl is a large bird, sometimes stretching 10 feet (3 m) from the top of its head to the tip of its long tail.

green peafowl lives in the dry forests of eastern Cambodia. These birds have shiny green feathers on the head and long feathers on the back that they open in a fanlike display.

Among Cambodia's best-known bird species is the greater flamingo. Adults are a beautiful rosy-pink color, with a slightly darker shade on the legs and the beak. The beak also has a decidedly dark tip, as if the bird dipped its bill into black paint. The greater flamingo is the largest member of the flamingo family, with an average adult height of about 52 inches (132 cm). In Cambodia, it is usually found along the coast feeding in shallow waters. Much of its diet is made up of small shellfish such as shrimp, mussels, and mollusks. The adult female lays just one egg each year, which she protects in a muddy nest.

One of the nation's rarest species is the Cambodian tailorbird. It was discovered as recently as 2009 and confirmed as a unique species four years later. It is found only in a single area of scrubland along the Mekong River floodplain, and within Cambodia's capital city of

Cormorants and darters nest in a tree in the Tonle Sap Biosphere Reserve, a protected area vital to many bird species.

Phnom Penh. It is a tiny bird, no more than about 6 inches (15 cm) long, with a mostly gray body. The most outstanding visual feature is likely the rusty reddish-orange coloring on the top of its head. It is also known for its distinctly loud call. Despite being rare, the species is fairly hardy and able to live alongside humans. It seems to be able to nest almost anywhere it can find adequate cover.

When the king cobra is startled, it rears up and spreads its hood in an attempt to drive off predators.

Reptiles and Amphibians

There are more than 150 species of reptiles and amphibians in Cambodia. The tropical weather is ideal for these creatures, as they are cold-blooded and cannot regulate their own body temperatures. Due to the year-round warmth, they do not hibernate like some species in more temperate climates.

Many frogs live in the grasslands, forests, and wetlands of Cambodia, and new reptile species are still being discovered there. One of the most recent is a frog that is so tiny, it could sit on the tip of a person's finger. Another recently discovered Cambodian amphibian is much larger. It is a species of caecilian, legless creatures that look like large earthworms. Some grow several feet long.

Perhaps the most fearsome reptile found in Cambodia is the king cobra. This snake grows up to 18 feet (5 m) in length, and its bite can be fatal. Even longer is the reticulated python. This is the longest snake in the world, and some have reached more than 25 feet (8 m). It inhabits a variety of environments—everything from tropical rain forests to open grasslands—where it hunts mammals of varying sizes. A third dangerous reptile is the water monitor—a lizard that can grow up to 6 feet (1.8 m) in length. These creatures use their sharp teeth and claws both to defend themselves and to attack prey such as fish, rodents, snakes, and turtles.

Water monitors grow about as long as an adult is tall.

Native Toad

The Aural horned toad is an amphibian species that was discovered in the Cardamom Mountains in 2002. It lives only in Cambodia, and is believed to live only on Phnom Aural, Cambodia's highest mountain. There, it favors moist, humid areas with plenty of leafy coverage to help it stay out of sight of predators. Its brown color with dark lines camouflages it amid the leaves on the forest floor.

Fish

Nearly one thousand species of fish live in Cambodia's waters. About two-thirds of these are freshwater varieties, most being native to the Tonle Sap Lake and River regions. The waterways are filled with eels, rays, gobies, and sole. Saltwater species vary from brightly colored clownfish to large tuna.

One of the more interesting Cambodian fish species is the Mekong giant catfish. It gets its name from its remarkable size—adults grow up to about 8 feet (2 m) long and can weigh about 600 pounds (270 kg)—making it the largest freshwater fish in the world. It is generally harmless to humans because it does not have rows of sharp teeth. Adult catfish consume mostly algae, along with some plant matter. This species can be found only in the Mekong and its tributaries. It has become extremely rare because of both fishing and pollution.

Plants

Cambodia is home to nearly nine thousand plant species, including grasses, shrubs, and trees. Due to the nation's warm,

tropical weather, plants cover much of the landscape with lush greenery. In many of the forests, tall broad-leaved trees are interspersed with palms and bamboos. Vines creep up the trees, while grasses and shrubs cover the forest floor.

Hundreds of different tree species are native to Cambodia, but many are becoming increasingly scarce because of human development. Forests are cleared to make way for agriculture and construction, and trees are cut down for their wood.

Today, one of the rarest native trees in Cambodia is the Koh Kong palm tree. It is a small tree that grows to a maximum height of about 10 feet (3 m). Native only to the Koh Kong Province along Cambodia's southwestern border, it has a narrow, flexible trunk and produces many branches with literally hundreds of palms that are easily able to compete with low-lying shrubs for sunshine. It is found along rocky riverbanks, usually nestled among other plants.

Many different types of palm trees grow in Cambodia. Some remain low to the ground while others tower above the surrounding forest.

CHAPTER 4

Yesterday, Today, Tomorrow

PEOPLE HAVE LIVED IN WHAT IS NOW CAMBODIA for many thousands of years. This region's earliest inhabitants were hunter-gatherers. They gathered plants from the rich forests and hunted for meat. There is evidence of toolmaking from around nine to eleven thousand years ago. They also developed basic agricultural techniques and learned to domesticate animals. Early agriculture in the region was limited to items such as wheat and millet, and farm animals included goats and sheep, and later, cows and pigs. Over time, the people began making improved tools and weapons from stone, wood, and other materials. They also began making pottery, which they used to store food. Some groups moved to different locations depending on the season, using the same sites over and over.

Opposite: **An image depicting a Khmer army is carved into a twelfth-century temple at Angkor Thom, near Siem Reap.**

By two thousand years ago, rice production had become important in Cambodia. The people had also become excellent fishers. In this period, the people of Cambodia began exploring more distant regions and came into contact with peoples of other areas, including what are now China, India, Thailand, and Laos. By about 1500 years ago, early Cambodians had developed unique religious customs, formed rudimentary governments, and begun forging languages that would lay the foundation for those used today.

Archaeologists have unearthed troves of ancient artifacts in Cambodia. Some of the pottery dates back three thousand years.

One Millennium, Two Kingdoms

The first significant political structure in the Cambodian area was that of the Funan Kingdom, in the first century CE. The Funan area was not just modern Cambodia but also parts of Vietnam to the east and south. The people of Funan developed irrigation systems that helped them produce great quantities of rice. Early cities bustled with trade, enticing people from surrounding areas to come and take advantage of the growing commerce. A robust trade economy developed. People from the coastal areas supplied people in agricultural zones with fish and other goods in return for rice, vegetables, and meats such as pork and beef.

The Phnom Da temple south of Phnom Penh was built about 1,500 years ago, during the Funan period.

Funan's urban centers also offered varied commodities such as gold, silver, timber, spices, and ivory. They served as meeting points for visitors from far-off places such as China and India, who brought not just their goods but also the customs and languages of their homelands. The Chinese and Indians,

Funan Kingdom

Funan, 250 CE
— Trade route
 Present-day Cambodia

for example, brought Buddhism and Hinduism to the region. In this respect, the Funan Kingdom became an early type of "melting pot" community. Funan also controlled many trade routes, giving it additional economic power.

Historians have argued, however, over the extent of Funan's political prominence. There is, for example, little evidence that it was ever truly united under one leader or government, acting with the impact of a unified political state. Some experts believe its influence reached as far as the modern areas of Myanmar, Malaysia, and Vietnam. Others believe it was merely a loosely run community that just happened to be in the right place at the right time to profit from the wider economy of the region. Historians also debate why its standing began to wane, sometime around the middle of the first millennium. It seems likely, however, that as other cultures sought fortunes elsewhere, trade routes shifted.

The area of Funan eventually became known as Chenla. It is likely that the region was divided into Land Chenla and Water Chenla. The people of Land Chenla, in the north, practiced agriculture, while those of Water Chenla, in the south, were more involved with trade. The Chenla period is renowned for its sculpture and architecture, particularly its stone temples. Chenla lasted perhaps two centuries before a new empire emerged that would set Cambodia's course for the next six hundred years.

The Khmer Empire

The beginning of the Khmer Empire, also known as Angkor, was marked in 802 CE by a ceremony led by Jayavarman II, the ruler of Land Chenla. Water Chenla had been claimed

Indian traders introduced Hinduism to Cambodia. Creatures such as the Garuda—a half-bird, half-human that appears in Hindu stories—are carved on the many Hindu temples built in Cambodia.

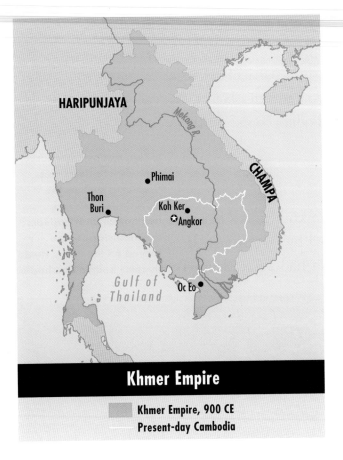

by this time by the nearby Malay and Javanese cultures, and Jayavarman II decided he would have supreme power over the remaining Chenla region. The years ahead were characterized by tremendous progress on all fronts. The Khmer made great improvements in technology, infrastructure, agriculture, and military power. Towns and cities were carefully planned, with construction of shops, hospitals, inns, bridges, roadways, and more. Extensive irrigation systems were put in place so people would have water for their homes and for use in agriculture, the economic engine throughout most of the Khmer age. This was also a time of construction of great temples and monuments. During the Khmer period, Hinduism, which had arrived from India centuries earlier, became the dominant religion.

At the peak of the Khmer era, in the eleventh century, upward of eight hundred thousand people lived in the area. Military forces were assembled not only to protect the Khmer Empire, but to also expand it. The area that would eventually fall under the Khmer rule was much larger than the area known today as Cambodia. It reached into what are now Vietnam, Laos, and parts of Thailand.

Angkor Wat

The Temple of Angkor Wat, the largest religious monument in the world, is the most visited historic site in all of Cambodia. Located near the city of Siem Reap, it is estimated that at least half of all tourists that come to Cambodia make a point of visiting it. The temple is famed for its grandeur, and for the complexity and detail of the sculptures that cover its walls.

The temple complex was built in the twelfth century. It was situated to face west, a traditional acknowledgment of death, since that is the direction in which the sun sets at the end of each day. This is somewhat unusual since such religious structures are usually built to face east, a direction of significance in many religions. Also unusual is the fact that the original temple was supposed to honor the Hindu deity Vishnu, but by the end of the thirteenth century it had become a Buddhist temple.

Jayavarman VII, the leader of the Khmer Empire from 1181 to about 1220, is considered one of the greatest Khmer kings. He brought new areas under the empire's control and had many temples, highways, and hospitals built.

Angkor served as the capital city from 802 until the mid-1300s. It was one of the most advanced cities of its time, and the ruins of its temples are a tremendous draw to this day.

The great Khmer period began to decline in the mid-fifteenth century. This was in part due to shifts in power in the surrounding regions. Siam (today's Thailand) and Vietnam, for example, grew in strength and influence and eventually warfare erupted. The Tai people (from present-day Thailand) attacked Khmer repeatedly. The Khmer continued to weaken, and in the 1800s, Siam and Vietnam fought for control of Cambodia. Eventually, the two gained joint control of the region.

European Control

Starting as early as the mid-1500s, France began claiming lands far beyond its borders. It took control of the distant areas of North America, Africa, and Asia, and began exploiting these lands and their resources, building the French colonial empire. In the 1800s, it acquired several territories in Southeast Asia, which became known as French Indochina and included parts of what are now Vietnam, Laos, and China. Then, in 1863, King Norodom of Cambodia signed a treaty with the French giving them control of Cambodia in exchange for protection.

In the 1850s and 1860s, French explorers and missionaries wrote about the abandoned Angkor temples, attracting adventurous visitors to the region.

The French eventually began improving Cambodia's infrastructure. They built roads and railways, improved water management and sewage systems. They also diversified agriculture to produce more than just rice. The French established rubber plantations and more corn and cotton were grown. Some of these goods were exported to France to be used in manufacturing. France also expanded the education system so more Cambodians could go to school.

Rubber was a major business in Cambodia during the colonial era. Here, sheets of latex, which are used to make rubber, are hung up to dry.

Although there were some improvements under French rule, many Cambodians resented the French presence. Additionally, some Cambodians thought that the Vietnamese, who were also under French rule, were treated better and had more opportunities than they did. This caused renewed tensions between Cambodia and Vietnam, and more anger toward France.

World War II and Independence

When France took control of Cambodia, it promised it would protect Cambodia from foreign enemies such as Siam. This was one of the central reasons Cambodia agreed to submit to French con-

Norodom Sihanouk

Cambodia's third-largest city by population, Sihanoukville, was named in honor of Norodom Sihanouk, the nation's king from 1941 to 1955, and from 1993 to 2004. Born in 1922 in Phnom Penh, Norodom Sihanouk was raised by his grandmother rather than his parents on the advice of an astrologer. He was a bright young boy who was both academically and athletically gifted. He had a particular flair for politics, and he became king while in his late teens. He served both as king and, briefly, prime minister toward the end of World War II. He gave up his throne in 1955 to his father. Norodom Sihanouk then became more involved in formal politics, fighting for constitutional changes that expanded rights for ordinary citizens, such as voting rights for women. He returned to the throne in 1993 and reigned until 2004. In the years that followed, he often commented on the state of political affairs in Cambodia. He died in 2012.

trol. And for the most part, the French kept their word in this regard. When World War II began, however, the French were quickly weakened by German attacks and could not protect Cambodia. In World War II, Germany and Japan were allies. Germany overran many European nations, including France. And Japan successfully invaded many of its Asian neighbors, including Cambodia.

Prior to the war, many Cambodians hated that their nation was colonized and resented French rule. The idea of independence was spreading throughout colonized areas of Southeast Asia, and many Cambodians were urging that their country

During the Vietnam War, supplies intended to help the North Vietnamese were carried on a jungle route through Cambodia and Vietnam called the Ho Chi Minh Trail (above). The Sihanouk Trail was a similar route used to bring supplies to the South Vietnamese.

become independent. After the war ended in 1945, France tried to maintain its position in Cambodia, but resistance proved too great. In a few years, French influence on the region had all but vanished, and on November 9, 1953, France formally recognized Cambodia as an independent nation.

The years that followed independence were marred by turmoil at home and internationally. Cambodia's king, Norodom Sihanouk, became wary of growing tensions in the region, particularly with U.S. involvement first in the Korean War and then in the Vietnam War. The king did not want Cambodia to become involved, and he pledged his support for the United States only if no Cambodians would be injured or killed. To that end, he refused to allow the United States to use Cambodian land or air space, which angered American officials. This resulted in a significant weakening of Norodom Sihanouk's political standing, and in 1970 the military removed him from power. The new leadership, headed by his enemies and supported by the United States, took over Cambodia and renamed it the Khmer Republic.

The United States supported the nation's new government, headed by Prime Minister Lon Nol. In the Vietnam War, the United States fought on the side of the South Vietnamese, who opposed communism, against North Vietnamese forces, who supported it. Lon Nol and his government opposed communism and were fighting North Vietnamese troops who were in Cambodia, as well as a growing number of Cambodian communists. In 1969, the U.S. military began a huge bombing campaign in Cambodia, in an attempt to weaken communist Vietnamese forces based there. Bombs routinely rained down on the region until 1973.

Under the Khmer Rouge

Despite U.S. support of the Lon Nol government, its reign would be short-lived. In 1975, communist forces drove it out, established their own base of power, and renamed the country Democratic Kampuchea. This group was known as the Khmer Rouge. *Rouge* means "red" in French and symbolizes communism.

The communists quickly changed the country. They did away with private property and money. Schools and temples were shut down. People were not allowed to travel. Everyone was forced to wear the same clothes.

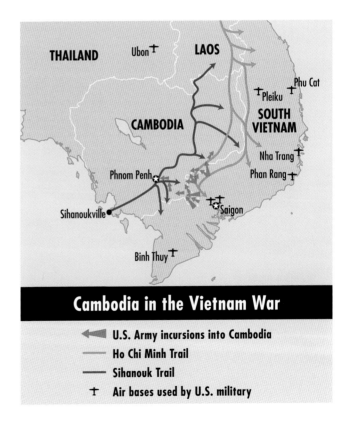

Cambodia in the Vietnam War

← U.S. Army incursions into Cambodia
— Ho Chi Minh Trail
— Sihanouk Trail
✝ Air bases used by U.S. military

Anything considered Western was destroyed. The Khmer Rouge wanted to create a new society by doing away with the old values. They wanted the country to start over again.

A small group of people controlled everything. In 1976, a man named Saloth Sar, who was known as Pol Pot, became prime minister. He would lead the nation through the coming brutal years. The cities were emptied of people. Nearly all Cambodians were forced to work on farms in an effort to double the production of rice. Many people died from starvation and exhaustion. Many others were tortured and killed because they were considered "traitors." In particular, educated people such

American planes drop bombs on Cambodia in 1973. Between 1969 and 1973, the U.S. military's massive bombing campaign devastated eastern Cambodia.

as doctors and teachers were targeted, as were ethnic minorities. The death toll was enormous. From 1975 to 1979, between 1.5 and 3 million Cambodians died. That amounted to at least 20 percent of the population.

After about four years of cruel oppression of the Cambodian people, the Khmer Rouge was forced from power by the Vietnamese military with the help of a Cambodian group called the Kampuchean United Front for National Salvation. They renamed the nation once again, this time the People's Republic of Kampuchea.

The deposed Khmer Rouge did not accept the situation quietly, stirring a bloody civil war that dragged on for more than a decade. This resulted in more than half a million Cambodians fleeing the country as refugees, and many thousands more being killed in the fighting.

The Khmer Rouge dumped the bodies of their victims in mass graves. A site near Phnom Penh where thousands were killed has been turned into the Choeung Ek Genocidal Center, a museum dedicated to documenting the horrors of the Khmer Rouge era.

The Modern Era

In 1989, the country was again being called Cambodia. By this time, world leaders had begun taking steps to establish peace in the nation. In the early 1990s, the United Nations, an international organization devoted to encouraging peace, helped iron out the details of a peace agreement and the basis for a more stable government that would include democratic elections for the Cambodian people. Free elections were first held in May 1993, with about nine out of every ten eligible voters taking part. Unfortunately, those ousted from power on both sides did their best to disrupt the elections and influence the outcome. Voters were intimidated in some places,

Cambodian refugees make their way into Thailand in the early 1980s to escape fighting between the Vietnamese and Cambodian militaries.

and blocked from casting their votes in others. Regardless, an elected government was put in place, and a new constitution for the country was drafted.

Today, the country remains unstable. But there are also hopeful developments. In 2009, tribunals were convened to mete out justice to key figures in the Khmer Rouge for the brutal treatment of many Cambodian citizens during their reign. Meanwhile, the economy is improving, as manufacturing booms and tourists arrive to view the country and learn about Cambodia's riveting past.

Warrior for Peace

One of the greatest heroes in modern Cambodia is a man given the name Eoun Yeak by his parents, but who has since become known to millions as Aki Ra. He was born in the early 1970s, and his parents were killed by Khmer Rouge forces soon thereafter. While still a small boy, Aki Ra was forced to act as a Khmer Rouge soldier. But soon after the brutal regime was forced from power, he joined the army of the People's Republic of Kampuchea. It was during this time that he was charged with the task of laying thousands of land mines. In the 1990s, he turned away from all violent practices and began taking part in programs designed to remove land mines from Cambodia and elsewhere. Once those programs ended, Aki Ra continued his work as a "deminer." He has also adopted children orphaned through warfare and other conflicts. A documentary about Aki Ra's life, *A Perfect Soldier*, was released in 2010, and in 2012 he was given the Manhae Foundation Grand Prize for Peace.

CHAPTER 5

Today's Government

CAMBODIA HAS A TYPE OF GOVERNMENT CALLED a constitutional monarchy. This form of government has a king who is supposed to adhere to the rules set out in the nation's constitution. In Cambodia's case, however, the king's position is largely symbolic. The person who actually runs the government is called the prime minister.

Apart from the monarchy, the basic structure of the Cambodian government is similar to that of the United States. Like the United States, it has three branches—the executive, the legislative, and the judicial.

The Monarchy

The position of king in Cambodia is largely a ceremonial post, with the king acting as the face of the nation. Though he does not wield much legal or political power, he can still influence

Opposite: **The Cambodian parliament meets in the National Assembly building in Phnom Penh.**

The Cambodian Flag

The Cambodian flag is distinctive—it is the only national flag that depicts a monument on it. The flag has blue horizontal bands on top and bottom, separated by a red band in the center. On the red band is a white image depicting temple towers of Angkor Wat. The blue symbolizes the nation's royalty, the red represents the rest of the nation and its people, and the white stands for the purity of religion. The tower structure symbolizes more than just a connection to the great Angkor civilization. It is also said to symbolize the structure of the universe as a whole.

The earliest known Cambodian flag, from the mid-1800s, had a design similar to the one used today. The current flag was adopted in 1948 and was used until

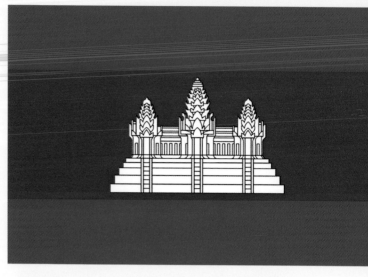

1970. Through the civil strife of the 1970s and 1980s a variety of flags were used. Then, in 1993, the 1948 flag was once again adopted.

his country. If the people regard the king positively, and he makes his positions on certain issues known to the public, he may increase public support for an issue, which can then affect the government's actions. So although the king cannot actually enact legislation, he can stir public sentiment to the point where legislators may be more likely to accept his position for fear of being voted out of office. And since the king's views can have an impact, he is often viewed by members of the government as a valuable adviser.

The Executive Branch

The head of Cambodia's executive branch is the prime minister. Although the prime minister is officially appointed by the king, the king is guided in this decision by the president, or

head, of Cambodia's National Assembly. The prime minister must be a member of whatever political party holds the majority in the National Assembly.

Norodom Sihamoni became king of Cambodia in 2004.

Cambodia's Prime Minister

Since 1985, Cambodia has had the same prime minister—Hun Sen, the leader of the Cambodian People's Party. Born in 1952, he initially planned on becoming a Buddhist monk. These plans were dashed, however, following the overthrow of the government in 1970. Hun Sen then joined the Khmer Rouge. In 1977, however, he went into Vietnam and took up arms against the Khmer Rouge, helping to defeat them two years later. At that time, he was given the post of deputy prime minister as well as foreign minister for the People's Republic of Kampuchea. In 1985, he became prime minister.

In the years since, he has been repeatedly accused of dealing harshly with political opponents, using threats and torture. Although he has sometimes shared the prime minister's power with other politicians, he remains the sole prime minister.

Once in office, the prime minister chooses other politicians to oversee different departments with different areas of concern such as health, defense, and commerce. Together, the leaders of these departments make up the Council of Ministers. The department heads almost always belong to the same political party as the prime minister.

The prime minister has the power to delegate his authority to any of his council ministers—or anyone in his government—as he sees fit. The prime minister also deals with foreign

A Cambodian Buddhist monk casts a ballot. Cambodians must be at least eighteen years old to vote.

Cambodia's National Government

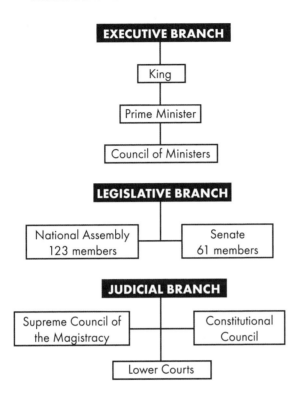

EXECUTIVE BRANCH

King

Prime Minister

Council of Ministers

LEGISLATIVE BRANCH

National Assembly
123 members

Senate
61 members

JUDICIAL BRANCH

Supreme Council of
the Magistracy

Constitutional
Council

Lower Courts

governments, forges diplomatic policy, oversees important meetings, and leads legislative initiatives. The prime minister's term lasts for five years, and there is no limit to how many terms a prime minister may serve.

The Legislature

The primary function of Cambodia's national legislature is to write new laws or make changes to existing ones. It is made up of two parts, the National Assembly and the Senate. The National Assembly has 123 members. They are elected

Sam Rainsy co-founded the Cambodia National Rescue Party, the second-largest political party in the nation. Cambodia's leading opposition figure, Sam Rainsy has twice left the country to avoid politically motivated arrest after accusing government leaders of corruption and other illegal activity.

through a system called proportional representation. People across the nation vote for the political party they support. Each party gets a number of seats in the National Assembly proportional to its national vote. For example, if a particular political party earns 10 percent of the national vote, its members will make up 10 percent of the National Assembly. Assembly members serve five-year terms.

The sixty-one senators are chosen in a completely different manner. Most of them are not elected by the Cambodian people, but instead are chosen by delegates from smaller government bodies around the nation, such as provincial and local governments. Two senators are chosen by the king, and another two by the National Assembly. Senators serve six-year terms.

In Cambodia, the executive branch of government is answerable to the legislature, and the legislature has the power to change the executive. If, for example, legislators disapprove of how the prime minister is handling the job, they can remove him from office through a two-thirds vote, called a vote of no confidence. The parliament can also pass laws without the approval of the king.

Political Parties

Cambodia has many political parties, although today only two hold any significant power. The most powerful by far is the Cambodian People's Party (CPP). Its policies generally tend to be conservative. The overwhelming majority of people in high government positions are members of the CPP, including the prime minister, the entire cabinet, and the bulk of both the Senate and the National Assembly.

Second to the CPP is the Cambodia National Rescue Party (CNRP), which is more liberal. It was formed in 2012 when other smaller parties combined. The CNRP is more concerned with the needs of ordinary Cambodians than the CPP is, fighting for personal rights and freedoms while combating governmental corruption. But with the CPP in command of a huge majority, progress for the CNRP has been difficult. It has made significant gains in elections to the National Assembly but is not represented in the Senate.

The Judiciary

The judicial branch of government is made up of a system of courts. The Constitutional Council determines whether laws violate the Cambodian Constitution. It has nine members.

The nation's highest court that reviews cases is the Supreme Council of the Magistracy. Below that are other courts. The courts are supposed to fairly and objectively handle legal matters such as criminal charges and lawsuits. But Cambodia's judicial system has earned a reputation for rampant corruption

Cambodians watch a livestream of the verdict in a trial of a Khmer Rouge leader. The trials have received widespread attention in Cambodia, and hundreds of thousands of Cambodians have observed them.

The Cambodian National Anthem

Cambodia's national anthem is entitled "Nokor Reach" ("Royal Kingdom"). The music was composed in 1939, and the lyrics were written about ten years later by Chuon Nath, a religious leader, poet, author, and musician.

English translation

Heavens protect the King.
Send him happiness and glory.
Us, your servants want you to reign
O heir of the Sovereign Builders
    and rule the Khmer Land and make it high
    and filled with honor.

Temples, hidden and asleep in the forest
Remembering glorious Moha Nokor.

Khmer is eternal like a rock.
We hope for the luck of Cambodia
The empire which challenges ages.

Pagodas, heard with songs
Remembering the holy Buddhists.
Let us be faithful to our fathers' faiths.
Hence, the heavens will help prosper
Cambodia, the Great Kingdom.

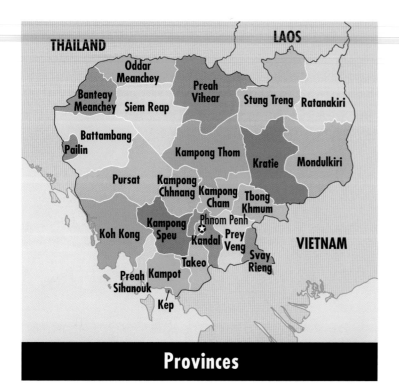

Provinces

and it is widely believed that it works in support of the ruling political party. The court has used fear and intimidation to control the people rather than working to protect their constitutional rights. Most Cambodians go out of their way to avoid becoming entangled in legal issues.

Administrative Divisions

Cambodia is divided into regions called provinces, which are similar to U.S. states. There are twenty-four in total, each with its own government. There is also a twenty-fifth division, Phnom Penh, the capital city, which is not technically a province, but operates as one.

Cambodia's provinces are further broken down into districts, one of which acts as its province's capital. There are smaller divisions as well, including towns and villages. Each division has its own governmental body, made up of elected officials such as mayors and council members.

Cambodia's smallest province is Kep, which has just two districts and is located in the extreme south along the shores of the Bay of Thailand. The largest is Phnom Penh, also located in the south, but closer to the nation's center. It has a population of more than 1.5 million.

The Cambodian Capital

The capital city of Cambodia is Phnom Penh, located in the southern region of the country along the Mekong and Tonle Sap waterways. The city was founded in the fifteenth century and became the Khmer capital following the downfall of Angkor. It would not become the formal capital city of the nation until hundreds of years later, in 1866. As many as two million people lived in Phnom Penh in the early-1970s. But during the Khmer Rouge regime, its population dwindled to less than one hundred thousand as almost everyone was forced to go work in the countryside. Many of its schools and museums were shut down.

Today, with a population of roughly 1.5 million, the city has rebounded and is the very heartbeat of the country. Phnom Penh is home to the nation's government and is a robust center of trade and tourism. Important museums include the National Museum, which houses a large collection of Cambodian art and artifacts, and the Tuol Sleng Genocide Museum, a former prison where thousands were killed during the Khmer Rouge regime. Phnom Penh is the meeting point for the nation's only two railway systems, and a transportation hub from which one can travel to almost any other town, city, or province. Its growth has skyrocketed in recent years, with a boom in the construction of hotels, markets, restaurants, and office buildings.

CHAPTER 6

Money
Matters

CAMBODIA'S ECONOMY HAS ENJOYED TREMENDOUS improvement in recent decades. This is due in large part to its transition in 1993 from a planned economy to a free-market economy. In a planned system, the government determines where people will work, how much of different goods will be produced, and how much they will cost. There is also a lack of competition that often leads to poor quality of goods. In a free-market economy, business decisions are made by the people who own the farms and businesses. They base their decisions on how much demand there is for different types of goods and how much of a profit they can make.

Soon after Cambodia's transition to a free-market system, its economy began to grow at a healthy pace. Then, during the worldwide financial crisis that began in 2008, Cambodia's growth rate dwindled to nearly zero, manufacturing and other

Opposite: **A woman sells doughnuts in Battambang.**

Farmers sell fresh fruits and vegetables at a market in Phnom Penh.

activities dropped, and workers by the thousands were left jobless. But since that period, Cambodia's economy has been growing, foreign firms are invested in the nation, and unemployment has dropped to historic lows.

Cambodian Currency

The basic unit of Cambodian currency is called the riel. Most people in Cambodia, however, prefer to use U.S. dollars when they buy and sell goods. Dollars are accepted almost everywhere. In fact, ATMs in Cambodia dispense U.S. dollars.

Riel banknotes come in denominations of 50, 100, 500, 1,000, 2,000, 5,000, 10,000, 20,000, 50,000, and 100,000 riels. Coins are in denominations of 50, 100, 200, and 500 riels. The banknotes all bear beautiful, colorful designs. The 500-riel note, for example, is cast in pink and gray and has an illustration of King Norodom Sihamoni on the front, with the Kizuna Bridge on the reverse. In 2017, 4,050 riels equaled US$1.00.

Agriculture

Agriculture plays a large role in the Cambodian economy. It employs about half of the nation's workers and constitutes an even higher percentage of its gross domestic product (GDP)— the total value of all the goods and services produced in the country. The most important crop is rice, which is both used at home and exported to other countries. Other major crops include cassava, cashews and other nuts, and soybeans.

Cambodian farmers also produce a broad variety of vegetables, corn being the most common. Popular vegetables include carrots, cucumbers, cabbage, and eggplant. Cambodians also

A farmer plants rice seedlings in a field near Phnom Penh. A lack of water can easily damage rice plants, so rice is usually grown in flooded fields.

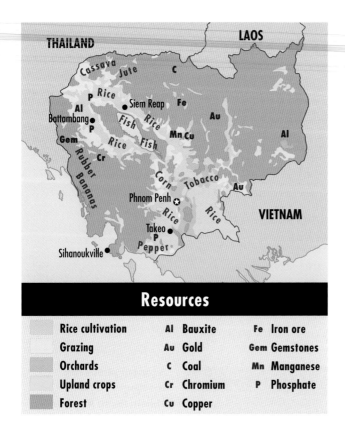

Resources

	Rice cultivation	Al	Bauxite	Fe Iron ore
	Grazing	Au	Gold	Gem Gemstones
	Orchards	C	Coal	Mn Manganese
	Upland crops	Cr	Chromium	P Phosphate
	Forest	Cu	Copper	

enjoy vegetables less familiar to some Americans, such as yard-long beans, chayote, and bok choy.

The most valuable nonfood crop from the agriculture industry is rubber. Cambodia has relied on the crop as an economic mainstay for decades.

Natural Resources

Fishing is also important to the Cambodian economy, and the Cambodian diet. Most Cambodians eat more fish than they do chicken or red meat. In the rivers, they catch fish such as perch and carp.

More than half the land in Cambodia is forested. Cambodian timber is used primarily in construction, although some woods are in demand by furniture makers.

Mining plays a small role in the Cambodian economy. Oil and natural gas were discovered in Cambodia in the 1950s,

Weights and Measures

Cambodia, like most of the world, uses the metric system for weights and measures. This system is based on units of 10. For example, in the metric system, the basic unit of length is the meter, which equals about 3.3 feet. One hundred centimeters equals 1 meter, and there are 1,000 meters in 1 kilometer (about 0.6 miles).

Cambodians sometimes also use other units of measure. They use Chinese measurements when weighing precious gems and metals. To measure gold, for example, most Cambodians use the Chinese tael instead of grams. One tael of gold is equal to 1.8 ounces, or about 50 grams.

but it is only in recent decades that exploration has begun in earnest. Gems have been mined in the southwestern region, and gold has been found in the central part of the country. There is some silver as well. Elsewhere, there are modest deposits of iron ore, manganese, chromium, and bauxite.

Another important part of the service sector of the economy is non-governmental organizations (NGOs). These are not-for-profit organizations that do humanitarian work. Some provide medical care, others are involved in education, or provide homes for orphaned children. Thousands of NGOs operate in Cambodia, and they account for a significant part of the nation's economy.

Rubber trees produce a milky liquid called latex, which is used to make rubber. A slit is cut into the rubber tree to drain out the latex.

Workers at a textile factory in Cambodia. Many factories in Cambodia are operated by Chinese companies.

Manufacturing

In recent years, Cambodia has become important in the clothing industry in Southeast Asia. So many foreign companies have invested in the Cambodian textile industry that very few textile businesses in Cambodia are actually owned by Cambodians. About nine out of ten textile workers in Cambodia are women. They have successfully lobbied for higher pay, but continue to suffer from poor working conditions and unusually long hours.

Cambodia has been trying in recent years to attract investments that would help it broaden its manufacturing base. The nation has, for example, improved roadways and railways to factory sites and shipping ports. People are learning the skills necessary to perform critical manufacturing tasks. Cambodia now has a few factories producing items such as electronics, machinery, and auto parts. Significant obstacles will have to be removed, however, if Cambodia is to have any chance for large-scale growth in the years ahead. Ongoing government corruption, for example, has made many foreign investors unwilling to commit funding to future projects.

Many roads in rural Cambodia turn to mud during the rainy season.

What Cambodia Grows, Makes, and Mines

AGRICULTURE (2013)

Rice	9,390,000 metric tons
Cassava	8,000,000 metric tons
Corn	927,000 metric tons

MANUFACTURING (VALUE OF EXPORTS, 2015)

Clothing	$5,916,280,000
Footwear	$637,000,000
Electrical equipment	$321,290,000

MINING (2012)

Sand	8,800,000 metric tons
Crushed stone	5,850,000 metric tons

A doctor examines a child at a hospital in Phnom Penh.

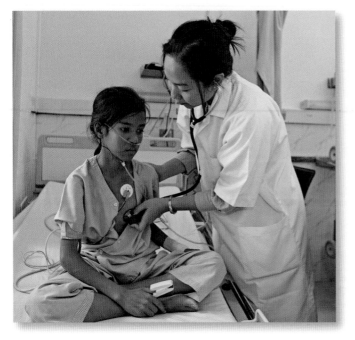

Services

Many people in Cambodia work in service industries. These are jobs that use a person's knowledge and experience but do not result in the creation of a physical product. Examples include barbers, waiters, and doctors.

The strongest element of Cambodia's current service sector involves tourism. In fact, tourism continues to be one of the nation's leading sources of income, respon-

sible for around a fifth of its overall GDP in recent years. Many visitors are drawn to heritage sites such as Angkor. Cambodia also possesses vast natural areas that remain pristine, drawing a large number of ecotourists, as well as many backpackers who want to travel as simply and inexpensively as possible. As more tourists discover Cambodia, the nation is investing heavily in improving tourism-based services, such as transportation systems, hotels, communication and banking services, and restaurants.

A common form of transportation in Cambodian cities is the *tuk-tuk*, which consists of a trailer pulled by a motorcycle.

CHAPTER 7

People of the Land

ROUGHLY FIFTEEN MILLION PEOPLE CALL CAMBODIA home. The overwhelming majority of them are Khmer people. Khmer make up more than nine out of every ten Cambodians. They are dominant throughout the nation except in the extreme eastern region.

Khmer communities have existed for thousands of years in certain parts of Cambodia. It is believed that the earliest Khmer arrived in present-day Cambodia as far back as 2000 BCE. By two thousand years ago, they were heavily influenced by Indian culture.

Today, in addition to Cambodia, sizable Khmer populations exist in both Thailand and Vietnam. Many Khmer also live in far-off lands, because people fled the region during times of violence. Many of these refugees went to France, England, Canada, and the United States.

Opposite: **Children play in the water behind a school on Tonle Sap Lake. Many buildings along the lake are on stilts so they won't be damaged by water when the level of the lake rises during the rainy season.**

Ethnic Cambodia (2013 est.)	
Khmer	97.6%
Cham	1.2%
Vietnamese	0.1%
Chinese	0.1%
Other	0.9%

The People of Cambodia

Cambodia has many smaller ethnic groups beyond the Khmer. The Khmer Loeu, who are closely related to the Khmer, live mostly in the eastern quarter of the country, with other pockets scattered along the borderland in the north and in spots in the west. About 150,000 Khmer Loeu reside in Cambodia today. They live in highland regions largely separate from the rest of Cambodian society. The Loeu are divided into more than fifteen subgroups and speak over a dozen different languages.

The Kreung are one of the many Khmer Loeu groups. They live in northeastern Cambodia and neighboring Laos.

Cambodia is also home to small numbers of Chinese, Vietnamese, Thai, and Lao people, mostly immigrants from surrounding countries. Other people belong to minority ethnic groups that have long lived in Cambodia. The Chams, for example, live in groups scattered through the country, including a related group of Mountain Cham along the easternmost border. Descended from sailors who arrived in what is now Vietnam from islands to the south around two thousand years ago, the Chams were once part of the kingdom of

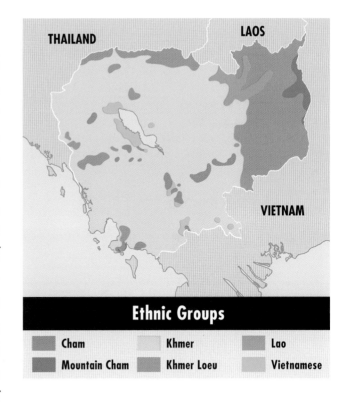

Ethnic Groups

Cham — Khmer — Lao — Mountain Cham — Khmer Loeu — Vietnamese

Champa in Vietnam. Many Chams fled to Cambodia when Champa was defeated by the Vietnamese ethnic group in the 1400s. Most Chams are Muslim, and they make up the largest Muslim population in the country. A smaller number of Chams practice Hinduism or Buddhism.

Rich and Poor

The rich and poor live vastly different lives in Cambodia. At the highest level are lawyers, doctors, bankers, and government officials. Many government officials are thought to be corrupt, enriching themselves as foreign companies invest in Cambodia. Although employment has increased in recent years, and many Cambodians find their lives slightly

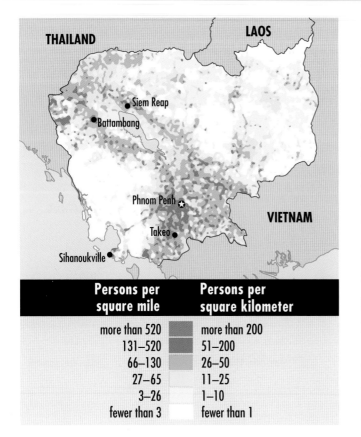

THAILAND		LAOS
Siem Reap		
Battambang		
Phnom Penh		VIETNAM
Takeo		
Sihanoukville		

Persons per square mile	Persons per square kilometer
more than 520	more than 200
131–520	51–200
66–130	26–50
27–65	11–25
3–26	1–10
fewer than 3	fewer than 1

Population of Major Cities (2017 est.)

Phnom Penh	1.5 million
Takeo	850,000
Sihanoukville	300,000
Battambang	250,000
Siem Reap	230,000

improved, the lives of the privileged have changed much more. Cambodia has developed into a kind of oligarchy, where there is a very small class at the top controlling the country, while the rest of the population is in poverty at the bottom. Signs of unrest and dissatisfaction are common, and other nations have urged the Cambodian government to address the issues of poverty and inequality.

The Lives of Women

In Cambodian society, women have traditionally been responsible for the home and taking care of the family. Additionally, they are also often in charge of a household's finances, which can bring significant power. Women usually have the support of their extended families, as they rarely move far away after they get married.

Most Cambodian women are able to speak freely, dress as they please, seek an education, and pursue a career. But there seem to be limits on how far women can rise in the society. Very few women in Cambodia hold high political office or run large businesses. The lives of women in rural areas are probably the most traditional, while women in more urban areas are more likely to get jobs and earn good incomes.

Education

Cambodia has seen a rise in formal education in the twenty-first century. During the depths of the Khmer Rouge era, virtually all educational institutions were brought to ruin and thousands of teachers were driven out of the country or killed. While there is room for improvement, the educational system is getting better. More than three out of four adults can read and write. Today, about 95 percent of all children enroll in school at the pre-kindergarten age.

A woman paddles a boat across Tonle Sap Lake. Cambodian women have a life expectancy of seventy-one years, four years longer than Cambodian men.

The school system is not standard throughout the country. A child may go to school four or five days a week for six hours a day in some places, and four hours a day six days a week in others. A student can expect to study as many as twelve subjects

A Cambodian child doing homework. Most Cambodian children attend elementary school, but the majority drop out before finishing high school.

A teacher leads a class in Pursat, near Tonle Sap Lake. Some schools in Cambodia require uniforms, but many do not.

in a single semester, with some subjects taught on certain days and not on others. In rural areas, teachers may sometimes not make it to school, so students simply return home. Children are encouraged to learn on their own, and many do so with help from relatives and neighbors. Sometimes teachers will earn extra money by offering private lessons in the evenings.

The current Cambodian education system suffers from many challenges. Most students complete elementary school, but less than half go on to high school. In large part, this is

University students read job advertisements at a career fair. Most of the top universities in Cambodia are in Phnom Penh.

because of the high level of poverty in Cambodia. Many older children need to work to earn money for their household. In addition, the education budget from the government is relatively small, and some of the funds are lost to corruption. With little money, schools often lack books and computers, and teachers' salaries are low.

Many Cambodian children, particularly poor children, attend school at Buddhist temples. NGOs also educate many of the nation's children.

Language

The Khmer language, often known simply as Cambodian, is the most common language in the country. It has more than 16.5 million speakers today and extends well beyond Cambodia's borders into neighboring Thailand and Vietnam, as well as smaller areas in Laos and China. It is an ancient language, which evolved from those heard in the civilizations of Funan, Chenla, and Angkor. It is also infused with Sanskrit and Pali, languages spoken in India.

Some walls at Angkor Wat are inscribed with ancient Cambodian writing.

The most common variety of the Khmer language is called Central Khmer, which is prominent in the central parts of the country. Regional variations exist, but people who speak different variations of Khmer can usually understand one another. Ethnic minorities in Cambodia who speak other languages often learn Khmer as a second language.

The majority of Khmer words have just one or two syllables. In the cases of words with more than one syllable, the stress is almost always on the last syllable. Khmer also places adjectives after the words they modify rather than before, as in English. For example, the phrase "red wagon" in English would be reversed in Khmer.

Khmer is written in a beautiful, intricate alphabet that is derived from an ancient alphabet used in India. This is just one of the reasons that the Khmer language is difficult for Westerners to master.

Cambodia has a large foreign population and a growing tourism business. Because of this, many signs are in both Khmer and English.

CHAPTER 8

Religious Life

THE VAST MAJORITY OF CAMBODIANS—ABOUT 97 percent—follow the Buddhist faith. Specifically, they are followers of the Theravada form of Buddhism. It is the most common form of Buddhism in the world, practiced by millions throughout southeastern Asia. It is the dominant religion not only in Cambodia but also in Thailand, Laos, Myanmar, and Sri Lanka. There are also many practitioners in nearby China, Vietnam, and Bangladesh.

Opposite: **A Buddha statue inside Angkor Wat. The temple complex was originally built as a Hindu center of worship but later became Buddhist.**

Buddhism

Buddhism does not prescribe any belief in a god or gods. Instead, Buddhists follow the teachings of Siddhartha Gautama. He was a philosopher who lived in eastern India some time around the fifth century BCE. He is more commonly known as the Buddha, which means "enlightened one" or "awakened one." Gautama taught his followers that they could reach inner peace by overcoming ignorance, anger, and the desire for worldly things—all traits that lead to suffering.

Becoming the Buddha

Siddhartha Gautama, the man who laid the foundations of Buddhism, is believed to have been born in either the fifth or sixth century BCE. He spent most of his life in eastern India. Many experts think he was born with considerable wealth, possibly even as a prince, but turned away from privilege and other worldly pleasures to seek enlightenment through a simple life.

At the time, some other religions encouraged their followers to indulge in physical comforts and pleasures. Gautama may have been repulsed by this, turning instead to asceticism, the practice of denying oneself any kind of comfort, in an effort to achieve a higher spiritual state. Over time, however, he concluded that compromise was better, a system known as the Middle Way. Through the Middle Way, people could enjoy the world and still maintain purity of spirit.

In Gautama's quest to end the suffering that arose through desires, it is said he sat under a fig tree and wrestled with his inner spirit until, finally, he overcame these weaknesses and emerged as the Buddha. Many Buddhists believe they know the exact spot in which he sat during this transformation, and it is considered a holy site.

In Cambodia, Buddhist monks wear orange robes.

Spiritual leaders of Theravada known as monks are visible members of Cambodian society. They wear long, simple orange robes and are held in high regard.

Other Religions

Islam is the second most common religion in Cambodia, accounting for about 2 percent of the population. The Muslim faith is based on the teachings of Muhammad, who lived from 570 to 632 CE and is considered by Muslims to be the last of God's prophets. Muslims, like Christians, believe there is only one true God, called Allah in Arabic. The holy book in Islam is called the Qur'an. It is a compilation of messages that God is said to have sent to Muhammad over the course of about twenty

Religion in Cambodia

Buddhism	97%
Islam	2%
Folk religion	0.6%
Christianity	0.4%
Nonreligious	0.2%

Cham Muslims pray at a mosque, a Muslim house of worship. Muslims pray five times a day.

years. The two main branches of Islam are Sunni and Shia, with Sunni being more common in Cambodia. The great majority of Muslims in Cambodia are of Cham or Malay ethnicity.

Less than one-half of 1 percent of the people in Cambodia practice Christianity. Regardless, Christianity is the largest religion in the world, with about 2.2 billion followers (more than a third of the earth's population). The fundamental principles of Christianity include the belief that there is one true God, and that the religion follows the teachings of God's only son, Jesus Christ, as related in the Bible's New Testament. Catholicism is the most common version of Christianity in

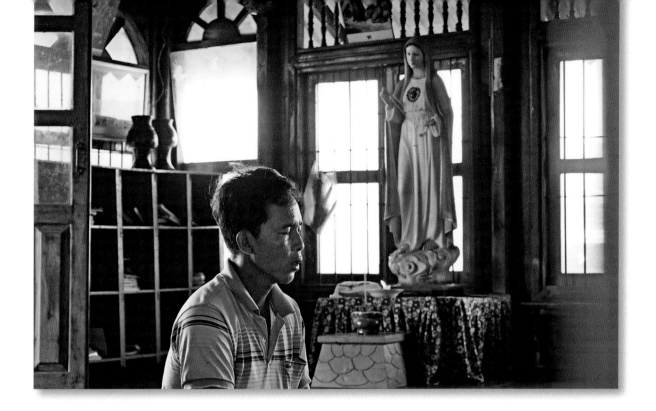

Cambodia. And in recent years, many Protestant churches have been growing in size.

A small portion of Cambodians follow folk religions. Most Cambodians who follow these religions live in rural areas. Some believe that physical things—certain objects, locales, and living animals—are endowed with a kind of spirit. They subscribe to the idea that agents of the spirit world are all around them, responsible for blessings such as health and happiness, and misfortunes such as illness. They believe that these spirits can be influenced by holy people, some of whom also possess healing powers.

A tiny fraction of Cambodians follow Hinduism. Hinduism is the most common religion in India, and it was common in Cambodia until it was overtaken by Buddhism during the time of the Khmer Empire. Many of the nation's greatest temples, including Angkor Wat, were built as Hindu structures.

A Cambodian Christian prays in a church. About twenty thousand Cambodians are Catholic.

A shaman in northeastern Cambodia leads a traditional ceremony. Many Cambodians practice both folk religions and other religions.

Government and Religion

The Cambodian Constitution guarantees religious rights and protections, and the Cambodian government maintains a policy of tolerance where religious faith is concerned. For the most part, this policy is honored, and Cambodians are free to worship as they choose. But this has not always been the case. During the Khmer Rouge period, religion was not tolerated. Buddhists, Muslims, and Christians were persecuted, and temples and mosques were destroyed.

Today, Buddhism is again the state religion of Cambodia. As such, the government recognizes Buddhist holidays, funds the building of Buddhist temples, and educates those interested in becoming Buddhist monks.

Religious Holidays

Two religious holidays are officially recognized in Cambodia.

Visak Bochea Day (left), which celebrates the birth of Buddha, falls in May or June. On this day in the morning, many people visit temples, bringing food for the monks. Late in the day is a procession. People carry candles, flowers, and incense.

In September or October is Ancestors' Day (below), which honors relatives who have died. During this holiday, it is believed that the spirits of the dead can return to visit the living. Cambodians visit Buddhist temples, bringing food for the monks, and also rice to throw into nearby fields to feed the spirits.

CHAPTER 9

Arts and Sports

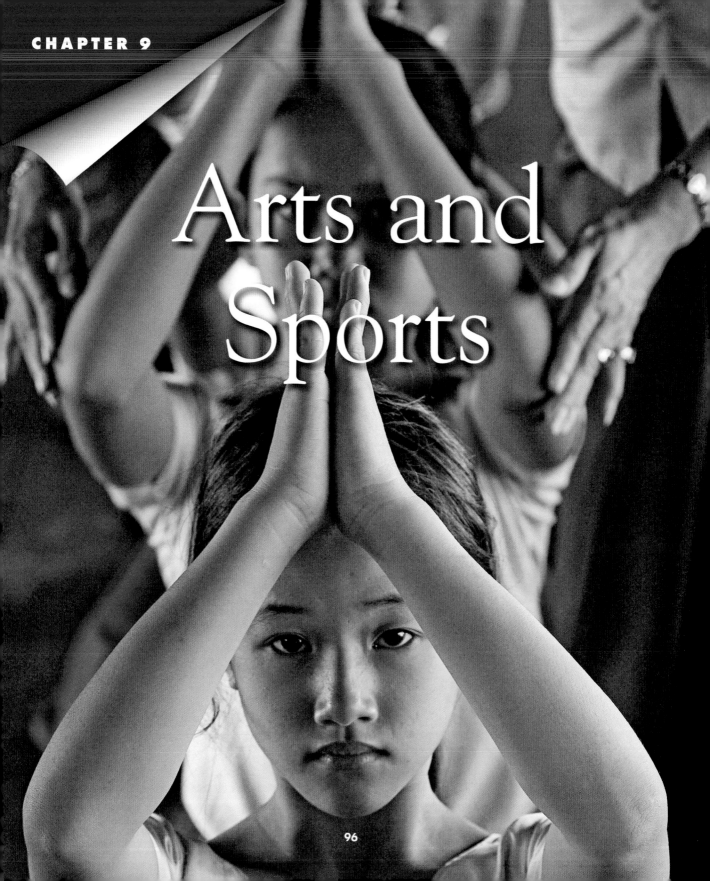

CAMBODIAN LITERATURE STRETCHES BACK MORE than a thousand years. The earliest examples are engraved writings on stone, often accompanied with ornate illustrations. The oldest known work in the Khmer language is the Reamker, the Cambodian version of the ancient Indian Ramayana epic. It is inscribed in temples throughout the country. Other early texts include poems, folktales, and historical accounts, as well as religious material, most reflecting the Buddhist or Hindu faiths. From around the 1600s, Buddhist monks wrote poems called *chbap* as a way of teaching young people the difference between right and wrong.

Early storytelling often involved royal figures such as princes and kings, and super beings like gods. These colorful tales appeared around the same time as the Buddhist morality

Opposite: **Girls learn classical Cambodian dance at a school in Phnom Penh.**

The Mon Prince and the Naga Princess

Cambodia has a rich history of myths and legends. One Cambodian folktale tells the story of a Mon prince and a Naga princess. Naga are dragon-like creatures that are important in stories from throughout Southeast Asia. This story dates back thousands of years, to the earliest times of the Khmer presence in the region.

According to the story, the Mon prince had heard of a beautiful land to the east that he could rule, but he had to get there by boat. So he set sail and soon reached an island with sandy beaches, lush trees, and sparkling rivers. He got off his boat, explored the island, and became tired. That night while he was sleeping, a group of young Naga people, who lived in a kingdom deep underwater, emerged from the sea to play on the beach. The Mon prince awoke to their noise and watched them from afar in astonishment. One woman in particular caught his eye, and he immediately fell in love with her. He revealed himself to the group, and the Naga woman of whom he was so enamored immediately fell in love with him. The woman's father turned out to be the king of the Nagas, and when he heard of his daughter's love, he was delighted. When the prince and the princess decided to marry, the king used his mighty power to draw all the water away from the land so they would have a place to rule. This new kingdom then became the nation of Cambodia, and the couple became its first royal rulers.

The story still resonates today. Some Cambodians like to say they are "from the Naga" or "born of the Naga."

poems and were among the earliest examples of literature to be read purely for pleasure. Some Sanskrit verses were written on sturdy palm leaves and survived for centuries.

Scenes from the Reamker adorn the walls of many temples in Cambodia.

Modern Literature

The earliest traces of modern Cambodian literature appeared in the mid-1800s. As in earlier Cambodian literature, moral themes were important. They came in the form of various poems, plays, and short stories. As these gained popularity, printed literature began to be mass-produced. Buddhist monks disapproved of this, because they believed that literature was a precious art form, not the routine output of printing presses. Buddhist texts were painstakingly handwritten and often included beautiful color images. The monks' influence was strong enough to slow the evolution of printed material in Cambodia compared to that in many of its Asian neighbors. Nevertheless, by the early twentieth century, Cambodian literature was being published in books, magazines, and newspapers.

The mid- to late twentieth century saw a rise in Cambodian literature. Cambodians wrote academic papers, popular non-fiction, and many novels such as mysteries, political thrillers, and historical romances. Literary output slowed to almost nothing during the brutal Khmer Rouge era of the late 1970s. During this time, a great deal of Cambodia's literary history was also destroyed. Since then, the agonies of that period have provided Cambodian authors with much to write about. Much of today's literature reflects the political and social struggles of

Shadow Puppets

One of Cambodia's greatest artistic traditions is shadow puppetry, or *sbek thom*. This tradition dates back about two thousand years.

In Cambodian shadow puppet theater, a light is directed toward puppets and performers, casting their shadows on a large white backdrop. The puppeteers are usually accompanied by a narrator and musicians as they act out stories such as the Reamker.

The large shadow puppets are made from cow leather. Artisans draw intricate figures on the leather and then cut them out to make the elaborate puppets.

The National Museum of Cambodia

Those who wish to learn more about Cambodia's cultural history should pay a visit to the country's National Museum. It is located in Phnom Penh, right by the Royal Palace. It was built between 1917 and 1920 and features a traditional terracotta design. Many of the items on display are sculptures, some dating back to the fifth century CE. One of the highlights is an eight-armed statue of Vishnu (one of the main Hindu gods) believed to have been made in the sixth century. There is also an Angkor collection with multiple sculptures of Shiva (another Hindu deity) dating from the tenth and eleventh centuries. In addition to sculptures, there are wooden boats, pottery, and ancient bronze pieces.

the country and is often concerned with personal freedoms, economic opportunity, and a nostalgic look at prewar days.

Music and Dance

As with its literature, Cambodia has a long musical heritage. Its music has absorbed influences from the many cultures that the nation has come into contact with. For example, around two thousand years ago, India's influence spread as far as Cambodia. Indian travelers brought musicians who were eager to share their talents. An ancient ocean port along the Mekong known as Oc Eo became a popular site where locals intermingled with foreign visitors. Musicians also came to Cambodia from China, Vietnam, Thailand, and, in time, European nations such as France.

Traditional Cambodian music often features gongs. The musician sits in the center of a circle of gongs and plays them with a mallet.

Along with these diverse musical styles came the need for diverse musical instruments. Some of the instruments used during the Khmer period include Cambodian versions of harps, gongs, small cymbals, shawms (woodwinds that look like the barrel of a musket), and drums.

These instruments also provide the music for Khmer classical dance. Many of these dances, performed with elaborate costumes, depict ancient stories such as the Reamker.

Today, Cambodian musicians fall into two categories: those who keep the nation's historic style alive, and those who embrace more modern trends. The former rely on traditional instruments such as xylophones, banjos, and drums, whereas modern bands take their inspiration from the radio or the Internet. Dance music is particularly popular, as are slower, soulful songs. It is not unusual, however, for even the most modern Cambodian musician to infuse his or her music with sounds reminiscent of Cambodia's past.

Classical Cambodian dance features stylized movement and precise gestures.

Visual Arts

Through the centuries, Cambodia's visual artists have worked with a broad variety of materials. The use of both stone and fabric, for example, dates back to the pre-Khmer days, nearly two thousand years ago. Textiles were woven using dyes made from natural sources such as tree bark. These colorful textiles were then used to produce clothing, tapestries, furniture, and other household items.

An artisan creates a textile out of silk. Cambodians have been producing silk for more than a thousand years.

Other common traditional materials include clay, gold, silver, and lacquer. Cambodian lacquerware was used to make both religious items, such as figurines, and everyday items, like bowls, plates, and cups. Lacquerware was also frequently made into decorative boxes that women used to store jewelry or spices and other dry goods for the kitchen.

The visual arts experienced a boost in the 1940s when the School of Cambodian Arts opened. Supported by the government, it gave rise to a new artistic movement led by some of Cambodia's greatest talents. Common subjects included the daily life of Cambodians, particularly in the areas outside the growing urban sprawl. The artists challenged themselves to

A variety of masks are worn in Cambodian classical dance. Masks of royal characters often have a single spire on top.

romanticize everyday life, a difficult task that was managed by such gifted artists as Nhek Dim. This growing movement ground to a halt during the Khmer Rouge period, and some artists—those whose work did not reflect the new regime's way of thinking—were killed.

The Art of Nhek Dim

One of the most renowned Asian painters of the twentieth century, Nhek Dim was born in a village in Cambodia's Prey Veng Province in 1934. His parents were wealthy landowners who had made much of their fortune through agriculture. When their son showed tremendous talent for art, they sent him to the School of Cambodian Arts, located in the capital city of Phnom Penh. Starting in the mid-1950s, he traveled abroad to continue studying and developing his craft. In the mid-1960s, he spent several years in the United States, at one point winning a cartoon contest sponsored by Walt Disney.

Beyond his art, Nhek Dim was also a skilled writer and musician. Even though much of his work featured neutral subjects, such as landscapes, portraits, and travel posters (right), he was targeted by the Khmer Rouge regime, and he disappeared in December 1978. His body has never been found, although there are persistent reports that he was murdered by Khmer Rouge forces near the border between the provinces of Takeo and Kampong.

Today, Cambodia's visual arts are once again thriving, although few artists manage to make a living with their craft. As Cambodians did in the past, these artists work in a variety of media. In recent years, Cambodians have produced paintings and silverwork and masks. Also seeing a rebirth in recent times is the creation of artistic kites. Kitecraft dates back many centuries and is enjoyed not only for the beautiful designs but also for the pleasure of flying the kites, a popular Cambodian pastime.

A Cambodian man flies an elaborate kite. Many Cambodian kites are equipped with a bamboo reed, so the kite "sings" as it flies.

Hem Bunting

Many of the Cambodian athletes who have gone to the Olympics have participated in track-and-field events. One of the most notable is Hem Bunting. Born in 1985 to a farming family in the nation's northeastern region, he was one of nine children, and they lived in tremendous poverty. Hem Bunting discovered his athleticism at an early age and focused on training as a way of rising above his difficulties. He became a distance runner and soon began competing in races throughout Southeast Asia, and then Europe. He repeatedly placed high in marathon races in the Asian Games, and even competed in the 2008 Olympic Games.

Sports

Cambodians, like people throughout the world, enjoy a variety of sports. Soccer (often called football outside the United States) is the most popular sport in the world and in Cambodia. It is an appealing sport because all that is needed is a ball and a place to play, so everyone can take part, even if they are extremely poor. Young people play in empty lots whenever they get a chance, sometimes late into the night under floodlights. The Cambodia national football team has been taking part in international matches since the country became independent in 1953. Fans flock to the National Olympic Stadium in Phnom Penh to watch the team play.

Sports centered on the martial arts also have widespread appeal in Cambodia. Some martial arts are based on skills that have evolved over many centuries. Bokator is one of the favorites. This complex sport uses both the body and weapons. It was developed for use by soldiers more so than athletes, and many people who practice it today wear the uniform of an ancient solider. Many of the positions and actions are based on those of animals. The participants use their hands and feet in a carefully choreographed array of close-combat strikes. Those who engage in bokator may spend years, even decades, learning its intricacies, as there are about ten thousand different movements involved.

Boys play soccer on a field in southern Cambodia.

Every bokator competitor wears a *krama* tied around the waist. The color of the krama indicates the level of expertise.

Khmer traditional wrestling has been popular in Cambodia for over a thousand years. It is reminiscent of the wrestling practiced in schools across America, but with some significant differences. Most notably, there is a dance performed before the match begins, giving the sport an artistic feel. The objective of Khmer wrestling is to drive one's opponent onto his

Cambodians compete in a Khmer wrestling match.

back. A typical match has three rounds. The winner of two of them triumphs in the match. The matches are accompanied by beating drums, adding to the excitement and tension.

The sport of chinlone is enjoying increasing popularity in Cambodia. Each team has six players. The object is to pass a small ball around using only the feet, knees, and head—very similar to the game known in America as hacky sack. One player goes to the middle of the field and begins kicking the ball into the air. He or she will often pass it to team members, who then have to return it with a single kick. Sooner or later the ball will fall to the ground, at which point that round is over. Chinlone is not a competitive sport in the sense that one team tries to score more points. Instead, winning is based on the arbitrary judgment of how elegantly the game is played. In Cambodia, chinlone is played by men and women of all ages. Adults and children often play together, too, creating a bond between generations.

Chinlone balls are usually made of rattan, a type of palm that is often used to make baskets.

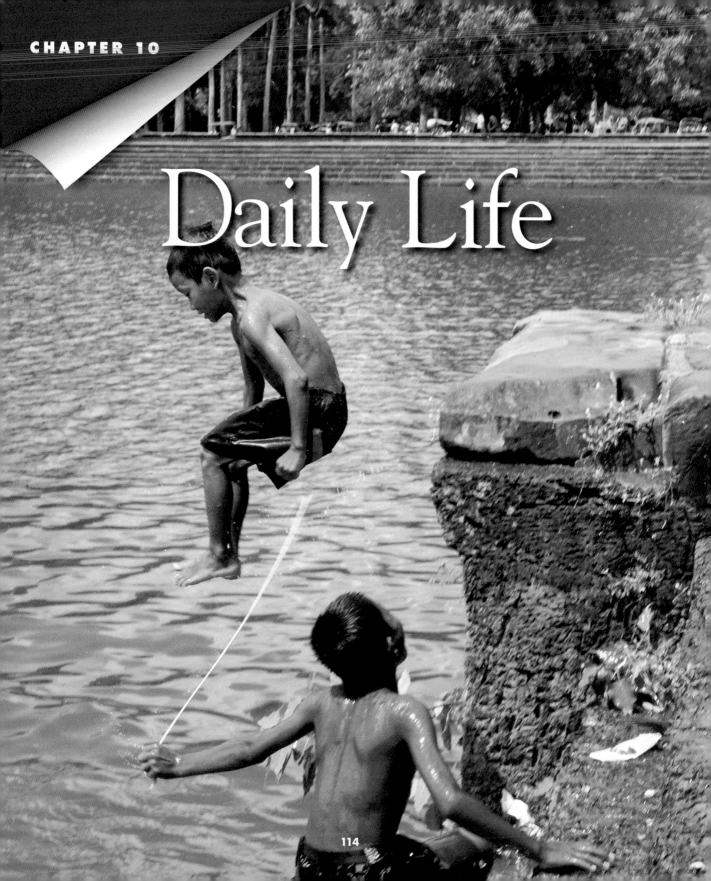

CHAPTER 10

Daily Life

DESPITE THE MANY CHALLENGES SUFFERED BY Cambodians in recent times, the nation's people are described by outsiders with words like *cheerful, kind, positive,* and *gentle.* They have tremendous pride in their country, and most are aware that their country is slowly moving in a better direction. In most towns, children run freely and safely, allowed to enjoy themselves while grown-ups keep a protective eye on them.

Cambodians also have great respect for one another. They take religion seriously, but rarely to the point where heated discussions erupt. Visitors have also remarked upon their unaffected nature. Pettiness and jealousy do not seem to enter their thinking. They are generally considered curious about outsiders, easygoing, and quick to help anyone in need, making Cambodia a welcoming place to visit.

Opposite: **Boys leap into the moat that surrounds Angkor Wat.**

A Cambodian man casts a fishing net into a lake.

Eating and Drinking

The staple food of the Cambodian diet is rice. Plain rice is a part of nearly every meal, including breakfast. Cambodians have developed many ways to prepare rice, and there are

The Game of Tres

A popular game among Cambodian children is called tres. It can involve one, two, or more players. Each player has a small ball, such as a tennis ball, and a pile of sticks on the ground nearby. The object is to throw the ball somewhere that it will come back—in the air or against a wall—with one hand, and gather up as many sticks with the other hand before it does. The sticks should be spread out to make the game more challenging. The player who gathers the most sticks is the winner. If there is only one player, he or she tries to top their own best score.

hundreds of different rice varieties at their disposal. Rice can be combined with meats and vegetables, steamed or fried, seasoned with herbs and spices, or served plain. Rice can be put into a soup or stew, or included in salad.

Grilled pork with rice is a popular Cambodian breakfast.

Cambodians also eat large amounts of fish, fruits, and vegetables. Pork, chicken, and beef are much less common. Many people do not buy fish. Instead, they go to the rivers, lakes, or sea and catch it themselves. Crawfish, shrimp, lobsters, clams, mussels, snails, frogs, turtles, and even crocodiles can end up on someone's plate.

People use many pastes and sauces in their food. These can be added to dishes for the sake of flavor and variety. Thus, it is not so much the food items themselves that make Cambodian foods unique, but the seemingly limitless array of flavors that are applied to them. One type of fish, for example, can be prepared in hundreds of

A woman shovels small fish to make *prahok,* a fish paste that is frequently used in Cambodian dishes. Huge quantities of prahok are made at the beginning of the year. The fish is cleaned, crushed, left out in the sun, and then salted.

different ways. Sauces and pastes are produced by blending different herbs and spices. Cambodia is located near some of the greatest spice- and herb-producing areas in the world, and as such has access to flavorful varieties rarely found in other countries. The same goes for fruits and vegetables, many of

Bananas in Coconut Milk

Fruit is at the heart of most Cambodian desserts. Have an adult help you make this simple but delicious dish using bananas.

Ingredients

2 cups coconut milk   8 ripe bananas

2 tablespoons sugar

Directions

Mix the coconut milk and sugar in a pan. Simmer the mixture on a stovetop over medium-low heat. Peel the bananas, and cut each one into three pieces. When the coconut milk sauce becomes thick, add the bananas. Cook until they are soft. Enjoy!

which grow well in the Cambodian climate. Fruits such as apples, pineapples, mangoes, watermelon, and papayas are common in Cambodia, as are the less familiar jackfruits, langsats, pomelos, and dragonfruits. Also known as pitaya, dragonfruit grows from small trees, is about the size of a small coconut, and has a vivid pinkish-red appearance.

Pomelos, jackfruit, lychees, and longans are among the many types of fruit common in Cambodia.

Fashion

During the Khmer Rouge period, people were not allowed to wear Western-style clothes. Instead, everyone was expected to wear plain black outfits, often called black pajamas. These consisted of black, collarless tops and loose bottoms, which created a look of uniformity among the population. The only variety in wardrobe allowed was in the choice of a garment called a *krama*, which can be worn around the neck as a scarf or around the head as a bandanna. It can also be used as a towel or as a sling to carry a child. Even krama were fairly standardized, with most bearing a simple checkered pattern. After the departure of the Khmer Rouge, Cambodian men and women embraced fashion styles popular around the world.

An elderly woman wears a krama, a traditional Cambodian scarf.

Today, the streets of Cambodia are filled with people wearing both Western-style outfits and traditional Cambodian clothes. One of the most common articles of clothing among women is the *sampot*, a single bolt of rectangular cloth that a

Most young Cambodians wear Western-style clothing.

National Holidays

New Year's Day	January 1
Victory Over Genocide Day	January 7
Meak Bochea Day	Late February or Early March
International Women's Day	March 8
Khmer New Year	April
International Labor Day	May 1
King's Birthday	May 13
Royal Plowing Ceremony	May
Visak Bochea Day	May or June
Children's Day	June 1
King's Mother Day	June 18
Constitutional Day	September 24
Ancestors' Day	September or October
Paris Peace Agreements Day	October 23
King's Coronation Day	October 29
Water Festival Ceremony (above)	November
International Human Rights Day	December 10

person wraps around the bottom half of the body. It is similar to the sarong worn by some Chinese, Indians, and others in eastern Asia. The manner in which it is arranged, as well as its colors and general design, can indicate a person's class and status. The origin of the sampot dates back to Funan times, when people wore them to please visitors from China. Although some men wear sampots, most favor loose-fitting trousers of silk or cotton. These materials are light on the body and help people endure the Cambodian heat. Men also frequently wear short-sleeve shirts untucked.

Everyday Etiquette

Cambodians tend to be formal with one another. They have developed a complex system of language and body language that varies depending on with whom they are interacting. The initial consideration is a person's rank, after which specific words and gestures are carefully chosen to reflect any differences in social status. People with more prestige, such as a doctor or a banker, for example, will be shown a greater degree of respect than a garment worker.

Cambodians often use a gesture called a *sampeah* as a greeting. The sampeah involves placing the palms together in front of the chest as if in prayer and bowing slightly. The higher the hands are held, the greater respect that is shown. The depth of the bow also indicates greater respect.

Cambodians are sensitive about physical contact between men and women. Unless a woman is a family member or close friend or associate, a man must be careful about how he interacts with her. Two men or two women, however, can be more casual with each other.

The head is considered the most sacred part of the body. It is considered extremely rude to touch an adult's head. Similarly, the feet are considered the lowest part of the body. Pointing a foot at someone can by interpreted as an insult.

Family

In Cambodia, the family is not merely a group of relatives who share the same household, but rather a strong and reliable structure that extends into Cambodian society and impacts everything a person does. Children grow up seeing their grandparents, aunts, uncles, and cousins on a frequent basis. This greater circle of relatives is known as *bong p'on*.

Cambodia is a very young country. More than 90 percent of the population is under age fifty-five. In large part, this is because of the many people who were killed during the Khmer Rouge era. Elders are considered wiser and more experienced about the ways of life, and younger people show them great respect. When someone is in trouble, he or she can depend on family for help. When one family member achieves success in the working world, it is expected that he or she will help relatives do likewise. Thus, there is loyalty within a Cambodian family, and with that comes a strong sense of stability in a society that has frequently been unstable.

Few families own cars in Cambodia, but motorcycles are common. Entire families routinely ride together on motorcycles.

Family Customs

Just as family is considered important throughout most of Cambodia, so is the act of marriage (below). For centuries, the great majority of Cambodian marriages were arranged by parents, with little input from either the bride or the groom. Although arranged marriages still exist in Cambodia, they are much less common than in years past. A woman who does not wish to marry her parents' choice of man is free to say so, and couples who meet on their own usually just have to ask their parents to approve the match. The family approval is important because most Cambodians do not view marriage as being between two individuals, but between two families. Most Cambodian women marry somewhere between the ages of nineteen and twenty-five, while men are usually five to ten years older.

When a Cambodian dies, family members usually take the body home to prepare it for the funeral. The family members wash and dress the deceased, and then place the body in a coffin. Three to six days after death, a procession of family, friends, and Buddhist monks brings the body to a temple, where it will be cremated. Close family members may shave their heads as a sign of mourning. Many people also wear white, the traditional color of mourning. Some families bring the ashes home with them. Many others keep them at the temple, where the deceased will be closer to the monks, and to Buddha. As part of the funeral services, relatives often burn offerings, which are meant to help the deceased in the afterlife.

Timeline

CAMBODIAN HISTORY

The Funan kingdom begins.	ca. 0–100 CE
The Chenla kingdom rises.	ca. 500s
Khmer Empire is founded.	802
The Angkor Wat temple complex is built.	1100s
The Khmer are repeatedly attacked by the Tai.	1300s and 1400s
The Khmer Empire declines.	1400s
Siam and Vietnam fight for control of Cambodia.	1800s
France gains control of Cambodia.	1863

WORLD HISTORY

ca. 2500 BCE	The Egyptians build the pyramids and the Sphinx in Giza.
ca. 563 BCE	The Buddha is born in India.
313 CE	The Roman emperor Constantine legalizes Christianity.
610	The Prophet Muhammad begins preaching a new religion called Islam.
1054	The Eastern (Orthodox) and Western (Roman Catholic) Churches break apart.
1095	The Crusades begin.
1215	King John seals the Magna Carta.
1300s	The Renaissance begins in Italy.
1347	The plague sweeps through Europe.
1453	Ottoman Turks capture Constantinople, conquering the Byzantine Empire.
1492	Columbus arrives in North America.
1500s	Reformers break away from the Catholic Church, and Protestantism is born.
1776	The U.S. Declaration of Independence is signed.
1789	The French Revolution begins.
1865	The American Civil War ends.

CAMBODIAN HISTORY

1941–1945	Japan occupies Cambodia during World War II.
1953	Cambodia gains its independence from France.
1954–1975	Cambodian leaders support the United States in the Vietnam War, but refuse to lend aid.
1975	The brutal Khmer Rouge regime takes power.
1975–1979	Under Prime Minister Pol Pot, at least 1.5 million Cambodians are executed or die from starvation or exhaustion.
1979	The Khmer Rouge are driven from power. The country is renamed the People's Republic of Kampuchea.
1993	Cambodia holds its first free elections.
2009	Tribunals are established to try former members of the Khmer Rouge.
2012	Former king Norodom Sihanouk dies at age eighty-nine.

WORLD HISTORY

1879	The first practical lightbulb is invented.
1914	World War I begins.
1917	The Bolshevik Revolution brings communism to Russia.
1929	A worldwide economic depression begins.
1939	World War II begins.
1945	World War II ends.
1969	Humans land on the Moon.
1975	The Vietnam War ends.
1989	The Berlin Wall is torn down as communism crumbles in Eastern Europe.
1991	The Soviet Union breaks into separate states.
2001	Terrorists attack the World Trade Center in New York City and the Pentagon near Washington, D.C.
2004	A tsunami in the Indian Ocean destroys coastlines in Africa, India, and Southeast Asia.
2008	The United States elects its first African American president.
2016	Donald Trump is elected U.S. president.

Fast Facts

Official name: Kingdom of Cambodia

Capital: Phnom Penh

Official language: Khmer

National anthem: "Nokor Reach" ("Royal Kingdom")

Gulf of Thailand

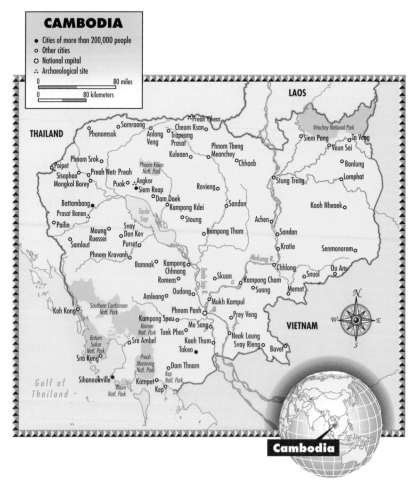

National flag

Kulen Mountain waterfall

Official religion:	Buddhism
Type of government:	Constitutional monarchy
Head of state:	King
Head of government:	Prime Minister
Area:	69,898 square miles (181,035 sq km)
Bordering countries:	Thailand to the northwest, Laos to the northeast, and Vietnam to the east, southeast, and south
Highest elevation:	Phnom Aural, at 5,948 feet (1,813 m)
Lowest elevation:	Sea level along the coast
Longest river:	Mekong, 2,703 miles (4,350 km) long, 302 miles (486 km) of which is in Cambodia
Largest lake:	Tonle Sap Lake, 1,042 square miles (2699 sq km)
Average daily high temperature:	In Phnom Penh, 95.5°F (35°C) in April, 87°F (31°C) in December
Average daily low temperature:	In Phnom Penh, 78°F (25.5°C) in April, 71°F (22°C) in December
Highest recorded temperature:	108.7°F (42.6°C) at Preah Vihear, on April 15, 2016
Lowest recorded temperature:	46°F (8°C) in the Emerald Valley near Bokor on May 13, 1967
Rainiest month:	September in Phnom Penh, 13 inches (33 cm)
Driest month:	January in Phnom Penh, 0.55 inches (1.4 cm)

National Museum

National population (2016 est.):	15,957,223	
Population of major cities (2017 est.):	Phnom Penh	1.5 million
	Takeo	850,000
	Sihanoukville	300,000
	Battambang	250,000
	Siem Reap	230,000

Landmarks:
- ▶ *Angkor Wat*, Siem Reap
- ▶ *Kep National Park*, Kep
- ▶ *National Museum*, Phnom Penh
- ▶ *Tuol Sleng Genocide Museum*, Phnom Penh

Economy: Rice is the staple crop. The nation also produces corn, cassava, rubber, and many vegetables. Manufacturing is a growing part of the economy. Textiles are the most common manufactured products. The country also produces electronics, machinery, food products, and wood products. Tourism is also playing an increasingly large role in the nation's economy.

Currency: The riel. In 2017, 4,050 riels equaled US$1.00.

System of weights and measures: Metric system

Literacy rate (2015): 77%

Currency

Schoolchildren

Hem Bunting

Common Khmer words and phrases:

joohm ree-up soo-a	hello
Sok-sa bai jee-a tay?	How are you?
joohm ree-up lea	good-bye
Laok ch'moo-ah a-vwai?	What is your name?
K'nyom ch'moo-ah . . .	My name is . . .
soam-un-jern	please
arkun	thank you

Prominent Cambodians:

Aki Ra *Activist*	(ca. early 1970s–)
Hem Bunting *Runner*	(1985–)
Hun Sen *Prime minister*	(1952–)
Jayavarman II *Founder of Khmer Empire*	(ca. 770–835)
Nhek Dim *Painter*	(1934–1978)
Norodom Sihanouk *King*	(1922–2012)
Pol Pot *Khmer Rouge leader and dictator*	(1925–1998)

To Find Out More

Books

▶ Keat, Nawuth, and Martha Kendall. *Alive in the Killing Fields: Surviving the Khmer Rouge Genocide*. New York: Penguin, 2009.

▶ McCormick, Patricia. *Never Fall Down*. New York: Harper Collins, 2012.

▶ Sobol, Richard. *The Mysteries of Angkor Wat*. Somerville, MA: Candlewick, 2011.

Music

▶ *Cambodia: Royal Music*. Paris: UNESCO, 1989.

▶ *Don't Think I've Forgotten: Cambodia's Lost Rock and Roll*. Atlanta: Dust-to-Digital, 2015.

▶ *The Music of Cambodia*. Tucson: Celestial Harmonies, 1994.

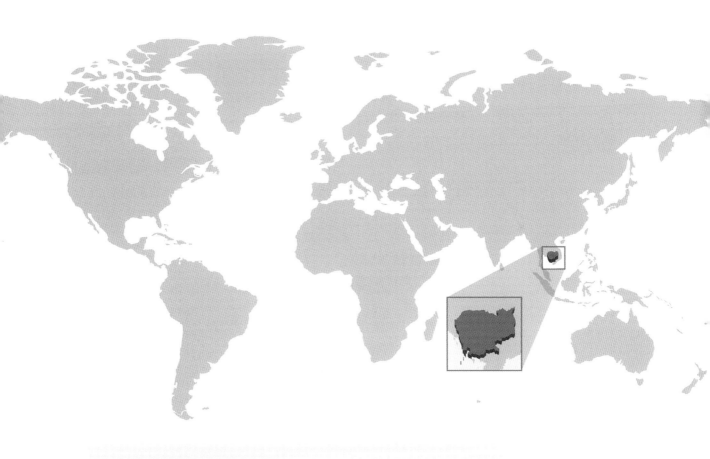

▶ Visit this Scholastic website for more information on Cambodia:
www.factsfornow.scholastic.com
Enter the keyword Cambodia

Index

Page numbers in *italics* indicate illustrations.

swimming, 76, *114*

China
Buddhism and, 39–40, 89
French Indochina, 45
Khmer language, 85
Mekong River system, 22
music, 101
sampot and, 124
textile industry and, 72
weights and measures, 70
Chinese people, 39–40, 77, 79
chinlone (sport), 112–113, *113*
Choeung Ek Genocidal Center, *51*
Christianity, 92–93, *93*, 94
Chuon Nath, 63
cities. *See also* Phnom Penh;
Sihanoukville.
Angkor, 36, 44, 65
Battambang, 20, 66, 80
Siem Reap, 43, 80
Takeo, 20, 80
civil war, 51
climate, 15, 22–23, 24–25, 32, *73*
clothing. *See also* people.
deaths and, 127
education and, 83
Khmer Rouge and, 12, 49, 121
krama, 121, *121*
sampot, 122, 124
Western-style, 122, *122*
coastline, 15, 17, *24*
communications, 12, 75
communism, 49, 49–51
constitution, 47, 53, 55, 94
cormorants, 29, *31*
Council of Ministers, 58
currency (riel), 68, 68

D
Damrei Mountains, 16, 18
dance, 96, 102, *103*, *106*, 111

Dangrek Mountains, 16, 18
darters, *31*
deaths, 127, *127*

E
economy. *See also* employment.
agriculture, 69–70
currency (riel), 68, 68
fishing industry, 34, 70
foreign investment, 72–73
free-market system, 67
government and, 67
growth of, 67–68
manufacturing, 53, 72–73
mining, 70–71
non-governmental organizations
(NGOs), 71
oil industry, 70–71
planned system, 67
rubber industry, 70, *71*
service industries, 74–75, *74*
textile industry, 72, *72*
timber industry, 70
tourism, 20, 21, 43, 53, 74–75
ecotourism, 75
education. *See also* people.
enrollment, 81, *82*
French colonization and, 46
government and, 13, 84
Khmer Rouge and, 12, 49, 51, 65
manufacturing and, 72–73
Phnom Penh, 65, 96
structure of, 82–83
uniforms, 83
women and, 80
elderly people, 125–126
elections, 52–53, 58, 59–60
elevation, 16, 17
employment. *See also* economy;
people.
arts, 108

education and, 72–73
etiquette, 124–125
foreign investment, 72–73
government and, 13
inequality and, 79–80
investment in, 72–73
manufacturing, *72*
service industries, 74–75, *74*
teachers, 9–10, 51, 81, 83, *83*, 84
textile industry, 72, *72*
women and, 80
English language, 87
etiquette, 124–125, *124*
European colonization, 45–46, *46–48*
European exploration, 45
executive branch of government, 49,
56–59, *57*, 61, 133

F
families, 9, 125–126, *126*
fishing, 11, 35, 70, *116*, 117
flamingos, 30
flooding, 23, *25*
flying foxes, 28
folk religions, 93, 94
folktales, 98
foods
Ancestors' Day, 95
doughnuts, 66
fish, 117–118, *118*
fruits, 68, 120, *120*
pastes, 117–118, *118*
pork, 117, *117*
recipe, 119, *119*
rice, 95, 116–117
sauces, 117–118
tourism and, 75
forests, *34*, 35
France, 45–46, *45*, 46–48
French Indochina, 45

Meet the Author

WIL MARA IS THE AWARD-WINNING AUTHOR OF more than two hundred books, many of them educational titles for Scholastic's school library catalog. He branched out into fiction in the mid-1990s, when he ghostwrote five of the popular Boxcar Children Mysteries. He has since authored more than a dozen novels, including *Wave*, which was the recipient of the 2005 New Jersey Notable Book Award; *The Gemini Virus*; and the *New York Times* bestseller *Frame 232*, which reached the number one spot in its category on Amazon.com and won the 2013 Lime Award for Excellence in Fiction. The follow-up to *Frame 232*, called *The Nevada Testament*, was released in 2016.

Photo Credits